HAPKIDO
ARTICLES ON SELF-DEFENSE
VOLUME ONE

SCOTT SHAW

BUDDHA ROSE PUBLICATIONS

First Edition 2012

ISBN-10: 1-877792-65-9
ISBN-13: 9781877792656

Library of Congress: 2012952245

Disclaimer. The author and the publisher of this book are in no way responsible for any injury that may occur by practicing the techniques detailed in this book. These techniques are presented solely as a means to aid in an individual's overall understanding of self-defense and are in no way a guaranteed to any individual's self-defensive readiness in a physical altercation. In addition, the physical techniques presented in these pages have the potential to cause injury to the participant. For this reason, any practicing of these techniques is taken at the practitioner's own risk. As the physical techniques describe within these pages may be too strenuous for some individuals, it is essential that a physician be consulted prior to any training.

10 9 8 7 6 5 4 3 2 1

Printed in the United States of America

Acknowledgements

Special thanks to:

Kenneth H. Kim, Vincent L. Spezze, and John Wells for helping to demonstrate the techniques presented in this book,

Joel Ciniero and Hae Won Shin for photographing the techniques presented in this book,

and to Jim Coleman, John Corcoran, Douglas Jeffrey, John Steven Soet, and Curtis Wong for their editorial and publishing support in the original presentation of these articles.

Foreword

The Korean martial art of Hapkido is an advanced system of self-defense designed to provide its practitioners with viable tools to defend themselves against even the most aggressive of attackers. Within the pages of this book are detailed in-depth understandings of Hapkido's self-defense arsenal.

The articles presented in this book were written by Hapkido Master Scott Shaw and were originally published by the most respected martial art journals in the industry. These journals include: Black Belt Magazine, Inside Karate, Inside Taekwondo, Karate/Kung Fu Illustrated, Martial Art Masters and Taekwondo Times.

These articles are presented as they appeared in the various magazines where they were originally published.

Table of Contents

HAPKIDO'S CIRCULAR THEORY OF DEFENSE

Many martial artists are under the misconception that the fighting system known as *hapkido* is derived from Japanese *aikido*. In fact, hapkido was developed by a Korean man named Yong Shul Choi in the early 20th century. In 1910, Choi traveled to Japan and studied *daito-ryu aikijujutsu*. Morihei Uyeshiba, who would later create aikido, studied at the same school Choi attended, and this perhaps explains the erroneous link between the two martial arts.

Upon returning to Korea, Choi integrated aikido's defensive tactics with the strong kicking and punching techniques of the Korean martial art *tae kyon*. Hapkido, therefore, possesses the deflecting maneuvers associated with aikido as well as the powerful blows of the Korean arts.

One of hapkido's primary principles is its "circular theory of defense." Instead of meeting an attack head-on, hapkido stylists believe it is far more effective to divert an opponent's force and turn his expended energy against him, while the defender conserves his strength.

The deflection of an opponent's energy is based on the "law of forward motion." By deflecting, for example, an opponent's punch or kick, yet allowing its motion to continue, you have caused your adversary to move forward under his own power Thus, your defense is virtually effortless.

To comprehend this concept more clearly, imagine an opponent throws a punch toward you. If you simply sidestep the attack and deflect the fist, the opponent will continue forward due to his momentum.

Once the opponent's strike has been redirected, you are in position to follow up with a counterstrike. This is central to hap-

The Shortest Distance to the Opponent is Not Always a Straight Line

by Scott Shaw, Ph.D.

1

kido's circular theory. What is the purpose of deflecting an attacker's blow if you don't additionally debilitate him so he cannot launch another technique?

The chief similarity between hapkido and aikido is that both styles use an opponent's incoming force against him. The primary difference between the two is that aikido is predominantly defensive in nature, while hapkido not only thwarts an opponent's attacks, but counters with its own debilitating strikes.

According to hapkido's circular theory, the defender should be able to flow effortlessly from one technique to the next, be they defensive or offensive maneuvers. The hapkido stylist is a continuum of energy as he shifts positions and quickly adapts his defensive strategy to his opponent's movements, searching for techniques that will facilitate the end of the confrontation. If, for example, the attacker throws a punch, the hapkido practitioner might deflect the blow with a circular inside-to-outside block, then counterattack by spinning and delivering a backfist to the opponent's head.

To better understand hapkido's circular theory of defense, assume a comfortable fighting stance and envision a circle extending approximately three feet around you. This circle is your range of defense and offense. If an opponent enters the circle, it is time to take aggressive action.

Literally translated, hapkido means the

In the hapkido circular defense sequence below, the hapkido stylist is grabbed (1) by the arms from behind. He quickly back kicks (2) his attacker in the knee, forcing the man to release his grip. The hapkido stylist then grabs (3) his foe's wrists, pivots (4), and moves (5) his adversary into position to be tossed (6) to the ground.

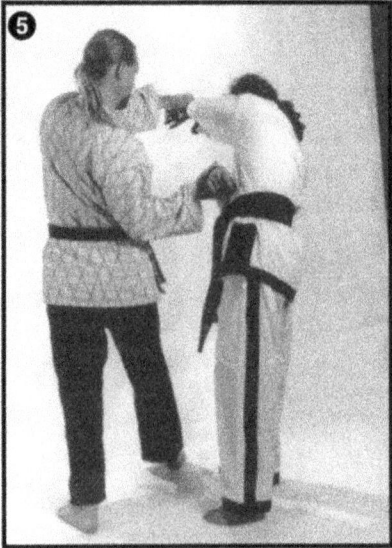

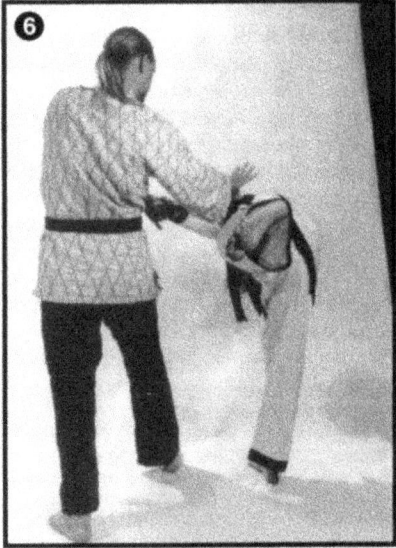

"way of coordination and internal power." This internal power, or *ki*, is linked to the hapkido stylist's physical and spiritual balance. Ki is developed by first gaining a strong physical and emotional balance in one's martial art. This balance is achieved by continuous focused practice and by coming to a deep understanding of every technique you perform. If any technique is misunderstood and performed incorrectly, it can easily be used against the martial artist by a competent opponent.

There are four key elements in hapkido's circular theory of defense: balance; deflection of an opponent's energy; focused strike point; and trapping or locking of the opponent's joints and limbs.

The central focus of hapkido's circular theory is balance. Without proper balance, a martial artist is at the mercy of his opponent. If you feel clumsy or awkward as you deliver a technique, you have not properly mastered it and should not be using it in a confrontation.

In the circular defense sequence at right, the hapkido stylist is grabbed (1) by the shoulder from behind. The hapkido practitioner quickly spins, grabbing (2) and locking his attacker's wrist, then follows up (3) with a knifehand strike to the ribs. The hapkido stylist then forces (4) his foe over his leg, knocking him to the ground.

The second element, deflection of an opponent's energy, protects the hapkido stylist from bodily injury. You can seriously injure yourself if you choose to meet an opponent's attack head-on. It will take a toll on your body, no matter how strong you may be. Diverting the opponent's energy is obviously a far wiser and less harmful defense.

Hapkido stylists do not grab or strike

In the circular defense sequence above, the hapkido stylist (left) deflects (1) an opponent's punch, turns and locks (2-3) his attacker's punching arm at the elbow joint. If necessary, the elbow can be broken at this point. The hapkido stylist continues to pivot, moving into position to throw (4) his opponent to the ground.

an opponent randomly. Rather, specific points on the opponent's body are targeted for attack. Some of the most common areas targeted by hapkido practitioners are the temples, nose, eyes, solar plexus and knees. Hapkido stylists do not want to trade blows with the opponent, thereby making the outcome of the altercation a simple matter of who is the strongest. Instead, they want to redirect the op-

ponent's attack and then follow up with techniques aimed at specific vital areas.

The fourth element in hapkido's circular theory of defense is joint locking and trapping techniques. The hapkido stylist who understands how an opponent's joints and limbs can be used against him can not only more easily redirect incoming blows, but also increases the number of calculated strike points at his disposal.

The quickest way to determine what will or will not work in a joint-locking situation is to experiment on yourself. Bend your finger, wrist or elbow the wrong way to experience the various levels of pain. When you manipulate an opponent's joints in a similar manner, you gain tremendous control over his actions and movement. It is just one more example of how hapkido stylists control and/or divert an opponent's energy to achieve a desired result.

Don't let the term "circular theory" of defense throw you off. Hapkido does include straight-line kicks and punches, but they are only utilized when such techniques become necessary.

Hapkido's circular theory of defense is designed to give practitioners an understanding of how to control and manipulate an opponent's energy, and then turn that energy against him to facilitate the end of a confrontation. It is not to be confused with Japanese aikido or even other Korean martial arts. Hapkido is a distinct and effective style. You would be wise not to leave home without it. ✄

About the author: Dr. Scott Shaw is a Hermosa Beach, California-based martial artist, actor and freelance writer who has a doctorate in Asian studies.

Go with the Flow

The principle of continuous motion

By Scott Shaw Ph.D.

O n a darkened street corner an unknown adversary attempts to punch you. Being a trained martial artist, you quickly block the attack and counter punch him. Your blow connects with his face. With this, you think you have accomplished your purpose and begin to walk away. Your opponent, however again charges at you. You do not see it coming, this time. He powerfully hits you. Stunned by the overpowering force of the blow, you are unable to continue the fight and completely at his mercy.

Once an adversary has accosted you on the street, counter attacking with one offensive technique is rarely enough, as can be easily illustrated by the average street confrontation. It is uncommon you will strike with enough force or power to completely disable your opponent in one blow. What the martial artist must do is find a conscious continuum from one self defense technique, onto the next and to the next until your opponent has no chance of coming back and defeating you. If you wait to see your opponent's responses to each hit you deliver it only gives him the ability to come back and attack you again, perhaps at that point gaining victory.

Though martial arts training generally teaches you to follow a block with a punch, a punch with a kick and so on, this is all too pretty; the streets are not like that. For your stylized techniques to be effective on the street your defense and offense must be extremely rapid and strike to the intended target with a continuous flow from one movement onto the next. This does not

Your opponent performs a straight punch at you (1). You quickly step in and block it with an in-to-out forearm block (2). You instantly perform a kidney punch (3). Then, kicking to the back of his knee, while locking his neck with a nose throw, he is sent back (4). On his way down, you lock his jaw with your hand and punch to his face (5). As he drops to the ground you deliver another punch (6).

mean you simply block and then strike once. What this entails is that you block your opponent's advance and then strike and continue on with another strike and another one, until he has become completely disabled.

Though this may sound logical to you, it is not as easily effectuated as you may think, for there are many elements that come in play in a street confrontation that do not exist in the martial art studio, certainly not the least of which is your opponent's desire to win. To this end, we must study the elements that make up the effective method of CONTINUOUS MOTION. Thereby making CONTINUOUS MOTION a science and not simply random techniques that are allowed to happen.

The five principle of CONTINUOUS MOTION:

1 Always follow one technique with another

2. Each defensive and offensive technique you perform must allow you to easily and effectively follow with another technique.

3. Always strike to the most debilitating and easily accessible target on your opponent.

4. Once your opponent has instigated the confrontation, you must assume that he has negative intentions in mind. Do not give him the chance to launch a secondary attack.

5. Never halt your attack until your opponent is completely subdued.

To view the five points of the CONTINUOUS MOTION theory we see that the foremost and most important point is the

first one; that one technique, be it defensive or offensive, is always followed by another and then another until you have obtained victory over your opponent. Furthermore, the key element to winning any street battle is to do whatever it takes to assure your victory over your opponent. Whatever striking technique you are sure will make powerful contact with your opponent is the appropriate one to use.

The streets are not a favorable place to be engaged in an altercation. What takes place there is neither pretty nor is it fair If you ever find yourself engaged in a street fight you must defend yourself at all costs as you can be certain your opponent will have no mercy on you. It serves no purpose, in the immediate disposal of the attacking opponent, to face him off and go blow to blow with him. This type of "fair fighting" is for the movies where the good guy always wins. In the street, any counter attack you unleash must be done with self preservation in mind.

To begin, we must first understand that CONTINUOUS MOTION does not mean your opponent and yourself go at it randomly, throwing whatever technique comes to mind, (as is generally the case in a street fight), until you both end up grappling like school children on the ground. What CONTINUOUS MOTION does involve is that you understand what type of technique effectively follows your last one; allowing you to maintain the advantage and thus accomplish your

objective of winning the confrontation quickly.

Though this is, in theory, the same sort of training most martial art schools teach; block this type of punch, with this certain technique, and then follow through with a strike with this leg or that hand technique. That type of repetitive training is all too sterile, however, and virtually is completely ineffective in a street fight.

In the streets, one technique rapidly follows another one. Whether they are launched with conscious understanding or not is irrelevant. If you do not immediately take control of a street confrontation, the random CONTINUOUS MOTION of your opponent will easily defeat the long trained martial artist, who believes in fol-

lowing the rules of combat as taught in the martial art studio.

The advantage the trained martial artist has over the avid street fighter when it comes to use the CONTINUOUS MOTION, is that they have developed the proper technique of the various martial art blocks, punches, and kicks. Knowing these techniques and then placing them in the scientific realm of conscious CONTINUOUS MOTION gives one the advantage in any confrontation.

You may, in fact, be quite schooled and capable of launching the appropriate block and following it will a powerful strike. The situation many martial artists fall into, however is when their first technique does not prove to be effective they cannot

Your opponent attempts a roundhouse punch (1). You block it with an out-to-in block (2). You immediately back fist him to his face (3), then deliver a knife hand to his groin with the same hand (4). You quickly continue through with an uppercut to his jaw with your other hand (5) and follow up with a straight punch to his face (6).

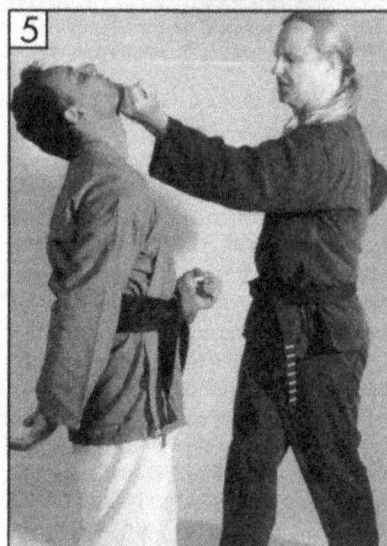

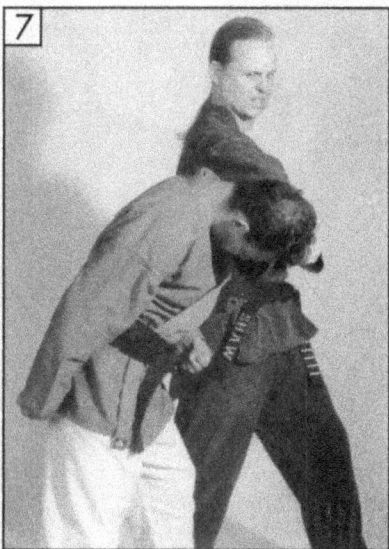

Your opponent attempts to back fist you (1). You block it with a double arm block (2). Immediately, while checking his striking arm you punch to his ribs (3). He then attempts to counter strike you with a roundhouse punch (4). You block it with an in-to-out block and straight punch him to the jaw (5). You follow up with a secondary punch to his face (6) and then an elbow to his head (7).

quickly and easily move forward into a secondary technique.

For example, your opponent takes a roundhouse punch swing at you. Quickly, you step in and block it with a standard in to out block, expecting to then counter strike. In a street fight it is very common that your opponent will, once his initial punch has been blocked, instantly swing at you with another random striking technique with his other arm. What will your course of action be if you have stepped in too deeply, placing all of your strategy on this one block and one planned follow-up? You will no doubt be clobbered by his second strike.

For this reason you must remain con-

tinually in movement in a street confrontation. Do not lock into one defensive technique and expect it to be enough to allow you to counter strike. Be constantly aware and willing to instantly change your defense strategy to overcome any specific fighting situation.

The second common mistake that you may make at the outset of a street confrontation is placing far too much emphasis on one very powerful offensive technique; assuming that it will cause enough damage to debilitate the opponent. What happens if this technique misses its target? A competent street fighter will take advantage of your miss and rapidly hit you. Here

9

again, you must never expect any initial or secondary striking-technique to win the battle for you. You must be willing to instantly change your mode of operations, at any point in the confrontation.

Do not lock yourself into the last technique that you have performed. By doing this you only prevent yourself from instantly unleashing a different attack when necessary.

For these combined reasons you must allow both your defensive and offensive techniques to be fluid, loose, and free enough that you can quickly move onto a secondary or further assault technique when and if it is necessary.

As a martial artist you have undergone much training in where to strike and why to strike there. By refining this understanding and making it street oriented, it will afford you the superior advantage in a street confrontation.

The obvious preliminary strike points, that will quickly debilitate your adversary are: the nose, eyes, temples, throat, and ears. The secondary strike points on an opponent are: his groin, knees, kidneys, and ribs. These are the only locations you should even think of launching an attack at during a street altercation. For to strike

Do not lock yourself into the last technique that you have performed.

randomly not only wastes your energy but gives your opponent the ability to take control of the confrontation.

Strikes should also not be aimed at your opponent's body, in a street confrontation, with the hope that with continual hits it will eventually have the effect of disabling him; as is sometimes the case in sanctioned boxing matches. This type of attack strategy gives the trained opponent too much time to launch a debilitating attack onto your person. Any strike you make must be very precise and be unleashed with a debilitating power to the primary strike zones.

You are not going to win a fight simply by blocking, as well. You can block and block but the opponent will continue to come at you until you debilitate him with a powerful blow. Make your movements count!

It is human nature once a confrontation has begun and any initial strikes have been landed that the losing opponent will attempt to take a hold of you and grab on tightly to your body. Thus, it is imperative in any street fight that you do not allow your opponent to grab you, lock your arms, or jump on you, sending you to the ground. For confrontations that end up in grappling matches are to no ones advantage; because the outcome is too hard to calculate and there are many disadvantages to being placed on the ground.

For this reason, to make CONTINU-OUS MOTION effective, it is to your benefit to keep yourself on your feet and keep your opponent from grabbing a hold of you. The easiest and most effective way to accomplish this is to keep your opponent at a slight distance, not allowing him to enter into a close enough range to grab on to you. The most effective method of accomplishing this is to immediately strike him the moment you are certain he means you harm. This first strike advantage is the absolute key to instant victory in any street confrontation.

At times, however the first strike is not always applicable or doable. Thus, the next step is to keep your opponent at bay, once the confrontation has begun.

The safe, yet realistic distance, is approximately two feet between your bodies. At this distance you are close enough to block, strike, or counter strike when the opportunity presents itself.

To achieve and then maintain this distance in a street fight, you must remain in constant movement, stepping out of the way of your opponent's strikes at each attack he attempts to make. Then, once the strikes have been avoided, you must move in quickly and strike powerfully once he is at the disadvantage of having just performed a failed technique. Thus, you remain in CONTINUOUS MOTION.

We must now come to an understanding of the dynamics of battle; of what, when, and where is the most rapid way of striking and thus debilitating the attacking opponent? As we have discussed the majority of the first strike points are to your opponent's head. Knowing this, what striking instrument reaches those point most quickly. Obviously your hands.

Therefore, straight punches, back fists, palm strikes and to a slightly lessor degree knife hands and elbows are the first strike weapons of choice in a street fight; as they are not only the closest to his head, they require a great deal less aim and timing then does a kicking technique to your opponent's head.

To be effective in a street fight, you must perform the strike which comes most naturally in any given situation. For example, if you have just blocked your opponent's oncoming punch, your hands are most likely at approximately shoulder level. What this tells you, is that you should continue through, telegraphing a fist strike to your opponent's head quite effortlessly. For by immediately striking to his head, once his technique has been blocked, not only does your arm not have far to travel but your opponent will have had virtually no time to redirect his energy to launch a secondary attack on you.

Furthermore, by instantly continuing through with a straight technique, such as a straight punch, you have not allowed your opponent the ability or time to see this type of technique coming. Thus, he will not have the ability to block it.

Punching techniques such as the roundhouse punch are much more pronounced and thus not often used by the conscious martial artists.

We now understand that a counter strike must immediately follow a block, in the theory of CONTINUOUS MOTION. And, the fist is no doubt the most universally appropriate strike weapon to deliver that counter strike with. This is due to the fact that not only does it possess the most power of all weapons of the hand, it also is the least likely to be injured once it has impacted its target. The fist, as well, takes the least amount of precise aim to injure your adversary.

Other hand techniques, such as the knee or palm hand possess a much greater risk of having the hand broken or injured at their point of impact then does the fist. As well, they must be much more calculated in their attack to be effective; they must strike a very specific target.

Once this initial penetrating strike has been made, the next strike must immediately follow.

In a street fight there is no guarantee that a target will remain in any location long enough for you to be able to deliver a powerful strike to it, as your opponent is continually in motion as much as you are. Therefore, though other hand techniques may prove to be effective as secondary strike weapons, the fist assures you of immediate powerful impact. For example, if your first assault does not make contact, the fist is easily redirected or formed into a secondary technique; be it a block or strike.

Once this initial penetrating strike has been made, the next strike must immediately follow. The secondary strike can be more creative as long as the opponent has been properly stunned by the first strike. Again, we must remember that it is unlikely your first strike will posses enough power to completely debilitate the opponent.

With this in mind, the reason you can vary your technique more at the time of the secondary technique, is that the initial stun of a powerful blow will last approximately three seconds. Though this may seem like a very small amount of time, in a street fight it can be the difference between winning and losing.

You must instantly follow up your first strike with an equally powerful blow to your opponent. This may well be accomplished by alternating arms and punching to his head again and again several times. You may, however, at this point have the ability to kick to the groin, or deliver a foot to his knee. The key element is to allow whatever fighting techniques will flow naturally and continually until your victory is assured.

As there is no time to think and plan out your strategy in a street fight, the blocks and strikes you make must become very natural and follow a flowing pattern. But, how can you achieve this ability, maintain control of a fight, and not allow it to become just a slug-fest? Though the answer to this is not simple, the ability to rapidly achieve desired results in a street confrontation comes from a tactical understanding of where and when to hit your opponent. Well protected partner practice is the ideal way to come to this understanding of how to effectively block and then immediately strike

The key element is to allow whatever fighting techniques will flow naturally and continually until your victory is assured.

while making all of your techniques very effective.

The most important factor of partner training, in relation to CONTINUOUS MOTION, is street fighting drills. Your practice opponent and yourself can not be allowed to know or expect what is coming; for this is the leading problem with most traditional martial arts training.

To become proficient in CONTINUOUS MOTION, it is important that while in partner practice you simply allow whatever will happen to happen, with no rules attached. This is the case in a street fight. From this type of training you can ascertain

what techniques will rapidly allow you to win a street fight.

The key things to remember in any street confrontation are: strike first before your opponent strikes. If this is not achieved, then block and instantly counter strike with the closest weapon you have to your opponent's head. This is usually a fist, but never rule out any other technique that may be effective. Then, once you have connected with your first strike, you must continue to strike again and again, to the most vulnerable region on your opponent, until he has no ability to recover and come back from your blows.

As martial artists, we must understand that through our teaching we may of course learn inner calm, meditation, and the like, but the term martial art itself means the art of warfare. To this end, we must also embrace the physical aspect of our styles and expand our martial knowledge to the point where if we ever need them, our martial skills will leave us victorious in a street fight. ⬛

About the author·
Scott Shaw, Ph.D. is an actor, writer, and martial arts instructor

Tae Kwon Do

Inside

December 1993 • K48324
U.S. $3.00 • U.K. £1.95
$3.50 in CANADA

Tae Kwon Do

Lessons in Leg Kicks
How to Blast Below the Belt

Muay Thai's Master Toddy

Scott Shaw

Exclusive!
The Throws of Korean Martial Arts

The Motion Philosophy of Street Defense

Five Awesome Defenses Against the Side Kick

CFW ENTERPRISES, INC.
20th Anniversary
1973-1993

0 71896 48324 6   12

Printed in the United States

13

The Motion Philosophy of Street Defense

You've been grabbed by an unknown assailant on a dark street in a deserted part of town. The thoughts of all the techniques you've learned in your martial art classes race though your mind. You come upon the one that should be used for this application. Instantly, you perform it and for some reason it doesn't work on your street-savvy opponent. Now what?

By Scott Shaw
Photos by Joel Ciniero

The leading mistake so many budding and even veteran martial artists alike make when encountering their first street fighting situation is, they believe they have learned all the necessary tools in their martial arts class to dominate any confrontation which may occur. This is often not the case; for it is not a controlled, fair fighting situation out on the street, as it is in the martial art studio. Your opponent in not going to grab you politely or exchange blows with you, and may the more points scored win.

Martial art schools may train you the proper techniques to perform in any given confrontational situation, but how often, in your school, has your training opponent truly resisted the blocking, joint-locking or throwing technique you have unleashed on him? With the type of sterilized training that goes on in most martial art classes, how can you expect the techniques you have learned to be fast enough and truly effective-enough to be a viable self defense tool on the street?

As our streets have become increasingly more violent and dangerous, to be a truly effective and competent martial artist you must go beyond what has been taught to you in the confines of the safe martial art studio environment. You

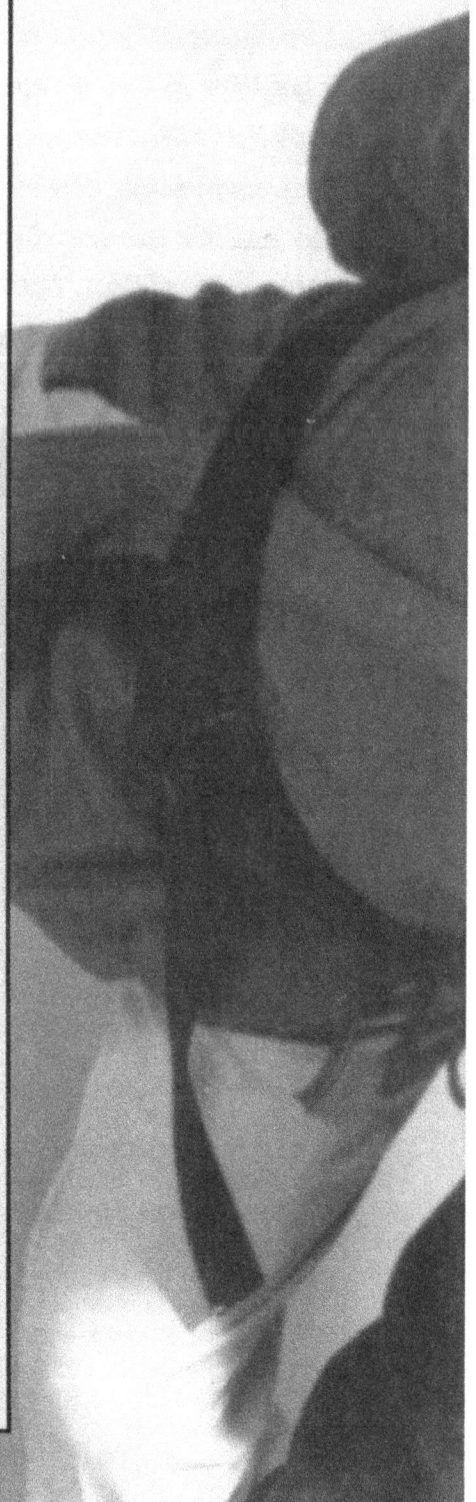

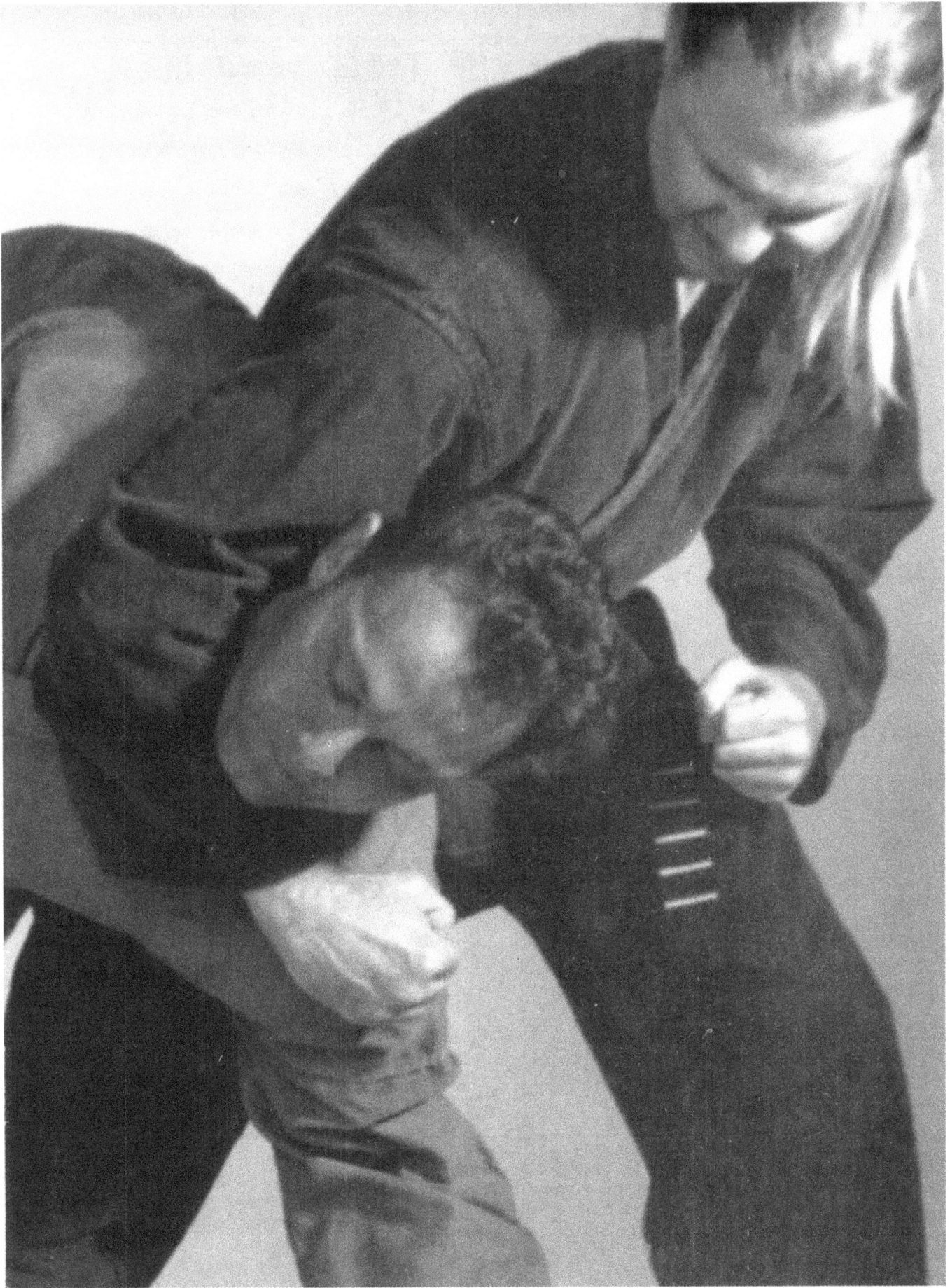

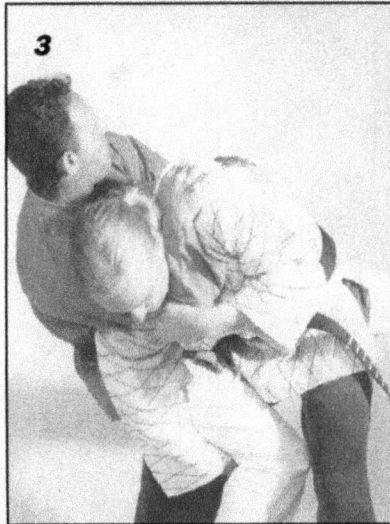

An assailant jumps on your back (1). Immediately, you elbow him in his ribs (2). Grabbing hold of his leg, you pivot (3) and throw your body on top of him (4). You then elbow him to his head (5). Instantly you roll over to your knee, gaining the superior position and strike him with your fist to his face (6).

"With the type of sterilized training that goes on in most martial art classes, how can you expect the techniques you have learned to be fast enough and truly effective enough to be a viable self-defense tool on the street?"

must consciously learn to defend yourself against any type of undefinable street situation that may occur.

Simplify Your Training

To do this you must take all of the stylized training you have received; and first and most importantly; simplify it. Then you must synthesis it, and place it in the realm of quickly usable and effective defensive and offensive techniques which you are certain will achieve your desired result on the street, which is to defeat your assailant. The only way to accomplish this is to work through all your fighting techniques with a trained partner who is willing to, along with you, take some hard falls and receive a few powerful strikes; in a controlled situation, of course, to define your own self-defense method.

To begin to understand the complexities of a viable self-defense for the streets, we must come to understand there is no definition out there on the streets. You have no idea what an opponent may or may not have the ability to launch at you. For this reason you must make any counter-defensive attacks very quick and very powerful.

To accomplish this, you must discard all of the non-effective defensive techniques you may have learned in your martial art school and learn, through continued practice with your training partner, what techniques are truly effective against each type of attack that may occur on the street — be it a strike, body grab, or chokehold. For without complete knowledge of a physical process that may take place in a true no-holds-barred street fight, martial art theory means nothing.

To become an effective street fighter you must make self-defense a science and thereby come to understand why certain techniques and the way they are applied are superior and more effective than others. We will call this self-defense science "Motion Philosophy" because through it, we come to truly understand the essence of confrontational movements. By putting "Motion Philosophy" to use, you will be able to physically implement the appropriate methods to defend against each type of attack which may occur and thereby save yourself and your loved ones from less than ideal situations on the streets.

"Work through all your fighting techniques with a trained partner who is willing to, along with you, take some hard falls and receive a few powerful strikes; in a controlled situation, of course, to define your own self-defense method."

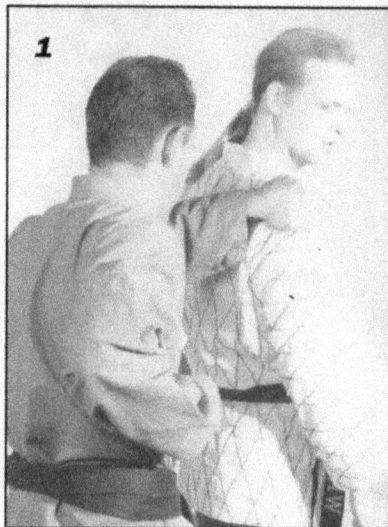

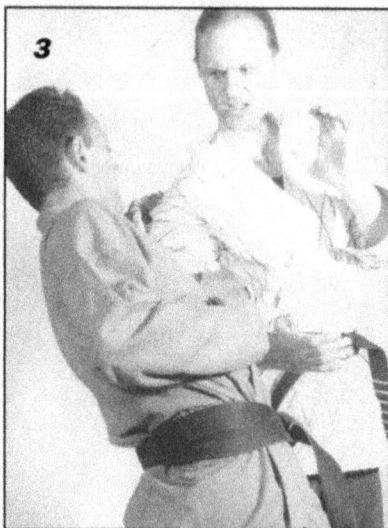

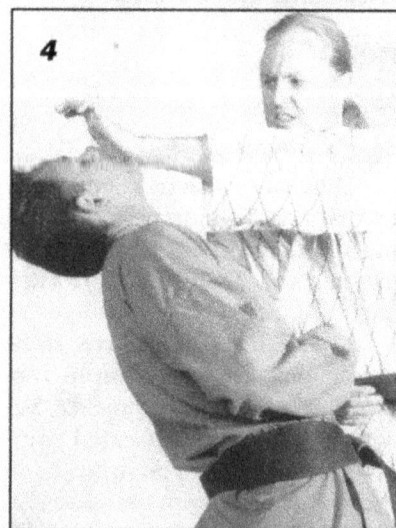

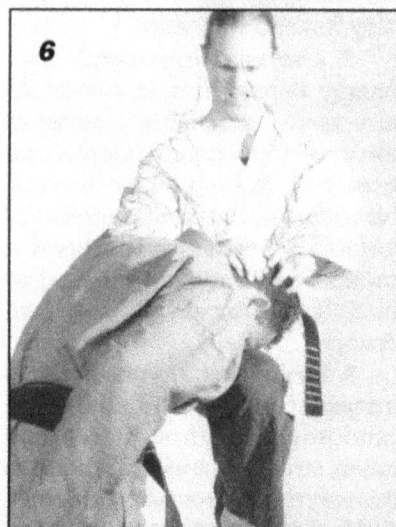

An opponent grabs you on your shoulder from behind (1). You swing your arm up and over his grabbing arm and bring it forcefully up (2), thus locking his elbow (3). You strike him in the nose with a palm hand (4). To maintain your advantage you grab behind his head (5), shoving it down as you knee him in the face (6).

18

> *"To keep your movements fluid and allow your opponent the least ability to gain victory over you, keep all motions, be they defensive or offensive, flowing continually from one and on to the next."*

Motion Philosophy

There are six steps in your own martial arts development that you must fully comprehend to be effective in a street confrontation. They are:

1. Keep all defensive techniques you use, very simple. Discard in theory and in practice, believing the very complicated grappling techniques you may have learned or have seen are effective. Anything to be effective must be very fast and very easy

2. Use your opponent's own energy against him. In any defensive maneuver, never attempt to force your opponent, in a street confrontation, in any path or direction his body does not easily or normally go in. By doing this, you use his own motion and momentum against himself, thereby saving your own energy

3. Strike first. If your attack is imminent and there is nothing you can do to get away from the confrontation, strike fast and strike hard. In this way the confrontation may well end before it has a chance to begin.

4. Counter strike. Immediately upon disengaging the hold of an opponent or moving out of the way of a first strike, always hit them before they have the opportunity to realign their energies and launch another attack at you.

5. Continuous motion. To keep your movements fluid and allow your opponent the least ability to gain victory over you, keep all motions, be they defensive or offensive, flowing continually from one and on to the next.

6. Range Effective. All techniques be they offensive or defensive must be easily executed. If you have to reach or stretch to gain access to your opponent with any technique, they are too far away for that specific technique to be effectively used.

The most effective method of street self-defense is to keep all defensive methods you use simple. This, of course, sounds very poetic, but how does one go about putting such a statement into a practical application that will work. The first step, though, of course, not always viable, is to not allow your opponent to hit you or grab you in the first place. This saves you from any possible initial injury and is much easier than you may think, if you can see the attack coming.

Your opponent attempts to punch at you or hit you with a weapon; by quickly stepping back out of the way, the strike misses. No doubt your opponent will be off balance due to the force of his own momentum and motion not connecting. You can now launch a very pow-

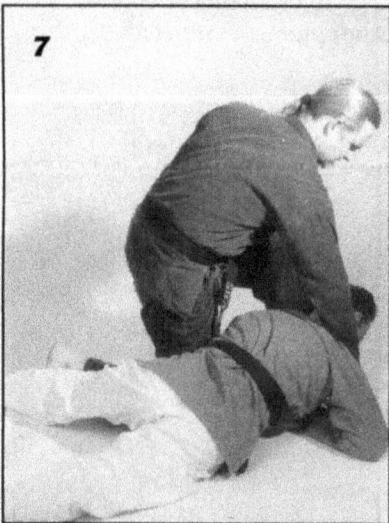

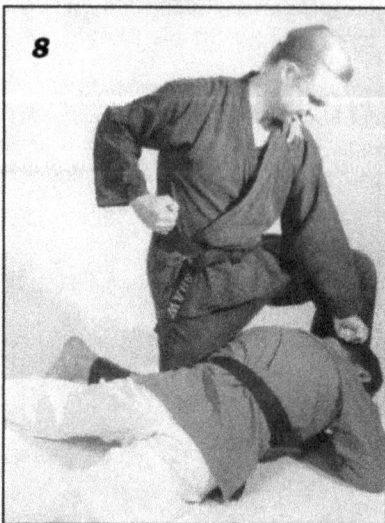

An assailant attempts to punch you (1). You sidestep and deflect the oncoming blow, thus avoiding its power (2). You immediately strike to his ribs, while your blocking arm remains in position controlling his arm (3). You continue through by locking his neck (4-5) and throwing him to the ground (6-7) where another hit can be delivered (8).

and perhaps continue with further offensive attacks on your body

The moment your body is grabbed is the time to instigate any defense technique. For at that moment, though your opponent is the aggressor, he is at his most vulnerable point of his attack; as he is most likely not expecting to be counterattacked so quickly

The first defense, if you know your body is in danger, is always an offense. Before you continue through, using the continual motion theory, to disengage his hold from you if it is possible always strike before any further defensive technique on your part or further aggressive technique on your opponent's part can be launched.

These strikes may take the form of an elbow to your opponent's ribs or head, if he has grabbed you from behind. It can be a groin strike with the knee or a palm strike to the nose, if he has grabbed you from the front.

erful counterattack when he is at this moment of vulnerability

This counterattack may include, but is not limited to a straight punch to his head, a front kick to his groin, a stepping side kick to his body, or a combination of these and other offensive techniques.

By keeping your defense very basic, you avoided being injured. You did not needlessly attempt to engage your opponent and end up grappling with him. You allowed the momentum he created by his own attack to be used against himself. Moreover, you were the first to strike the opponent in this scenario, thus, hopefully injuring him enough to alleviate any further confrontation from taking place.

A similar application applies if an opponent is attempting to grab hold of your body If you see this motion taking place simply by stepping from its grasp and immediately side kicking or back fisting the aggressor, again you simply moved away from the assault with no damage to yourself and gained the first strike advantage.

Breaking A Hold

Of course, it is not always this simple, what if an opponent does take a hold of your body or your clothing. The most important thing to do at these moments, is to instantly move into the appropriate action before the opponent has the ability to strengthen his hold on you

"As the majority of confrontations on the street end up in a grappling match, it is imperative that you study and master appropriate grappling techniques."

If he has taken hold from the side, a knife hand to his ribs or throat or a side kick to his knee may be appropriate. If the opponent has jumped on top of you and driven you to the ground, a strike to his elbow or a palm under his nose, may be the initial course of action. Whatever the technique is, it must be launched immediately; for this strike may end the confrontation and no further defensive technique may be necessary

As the majority of confrontations on the street end up into a grappling match, it is imperative that you study and master appropriate grappling techniques. If your opponent's grip on you continues

you must follow through with the most appropriate grappling defense that will free you from your opponent's grasp.

This may mean — if your opponent has grabbed onto a piece your clothing, at your shoulder level, from your back or side — pivoting and swinging your arm up and over your opponent's arm, and bringing it back under his, thus locking his elbow If he has launched a frontal attack upon you, your counterattack may entail a locking of his neck and throwing him to the ground.

The key element of all grappling encounters is, you must never attempt to force your opponent's body by trying to lift his weight, or to

control him by struggling against his muscles, while grappling with him. Only the loser of a street fight, attempts to fight body to body, muscle to muscle.

As a trained martial artist you must learn, through practice, to manipulate his forceful energies against himself. This is done quite simply by flowing with his motions. If he grabs you by the shirt and pulls you, simply by allowing his force to pull you forward while stepping behind his leg, then knife-handing him across the throat as you are pulled in, he has been injured and is probably sent to the ground.

As each encounter is defined by the opponent's movements, there is

You are forcefully gabbed on your shirt by your opponent (1). Immediately you elbow strike his head (2). Your striking arm continues through, reaching down and around his grabbing arm (3), as your other hand goes up and shoves the opponent back by his chin (4), thus throwing him to the ground (5) where, again, he may be struck (6).

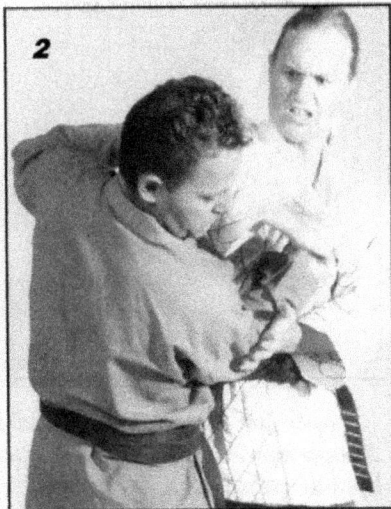

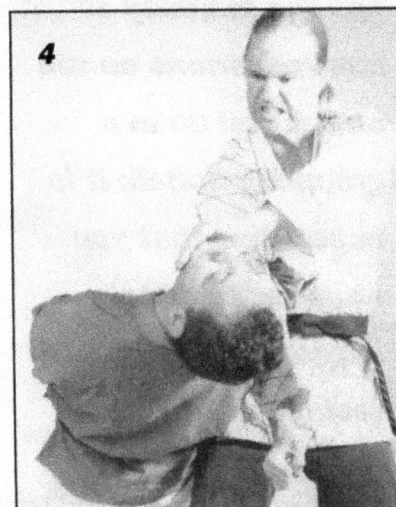

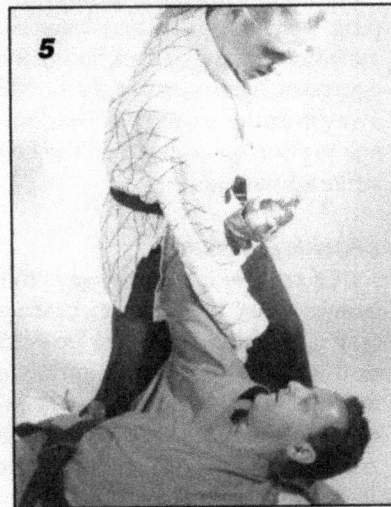

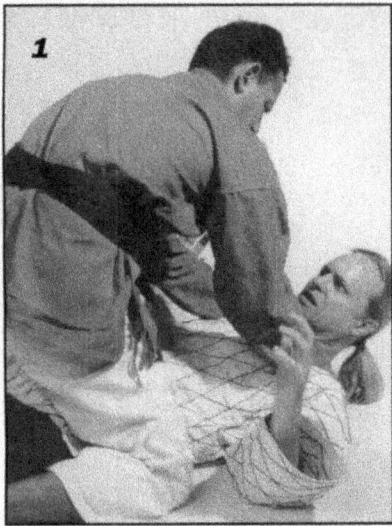

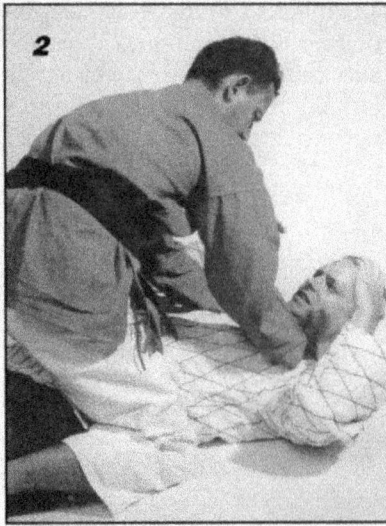

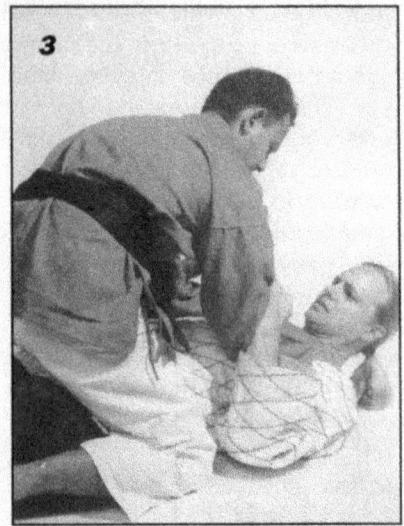

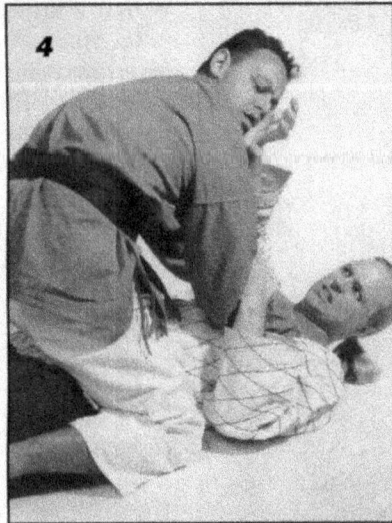

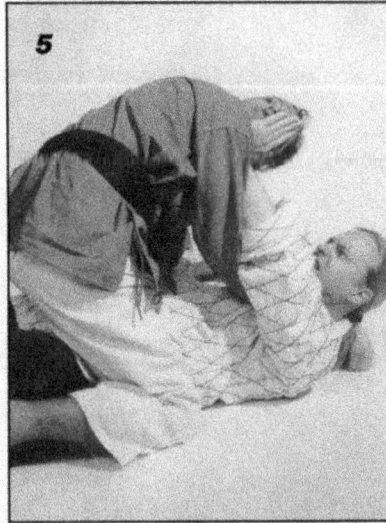

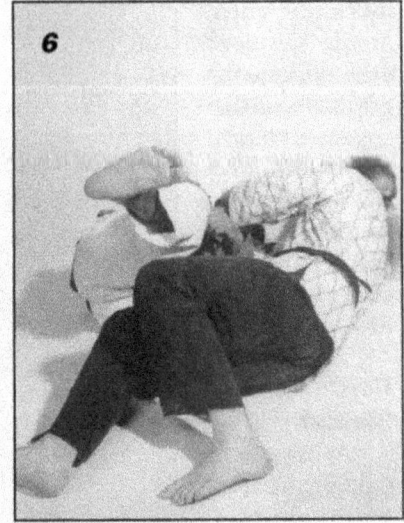

An assailant has you on your back on the ground (1-2). Using a knife hand, you simultaneously strike both of his elbows (3). You then reach up and palm strike his face (4). While this hand remains in place your other hand goes up, controlling his head (5) while locking his neck so he is thrown off of you (6). You then assent to your knees and strike (7).

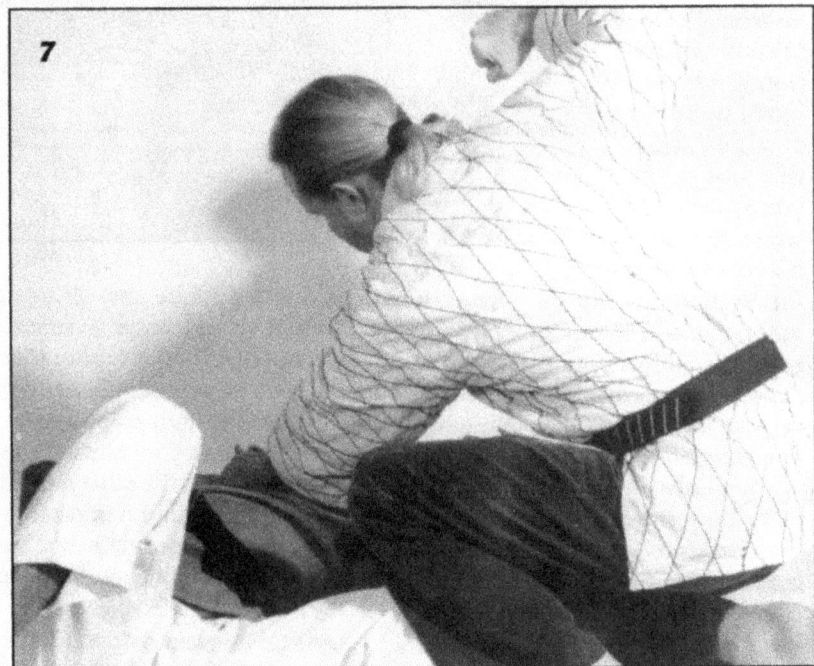

22

no hard and fast rule to answer what defensive grappling technique should be applied in every situation. The rule of thumb is, whatever gets you out of your opponent's hold most quickly and whichever technique allows you to easily counterstrike once this freedom has been gained. For that is the process of continual motion. Not only do you immediately strike your opponent once he has grabbed you, but you continue through with the appropriate grappling technique to free yourself from his hold if necessary Then, at the moment your opponent's grip has been disengaged, you immediately and powerfully counterstrike to keep him from attacking you further.

Continual Motion

In any street fighting situation you encounter, you must remain in continual motion. If whatever initial technique you performed did not work, you must rapidly strike again and move onto further techniques. For by remaining indecisive and in any one position too long, allows your opponent to have time to assess his next assault on you, that could take place while you stagnate in one location.

Not only should your mind and body be continually flowing from one conscious technique to the next but, as mentioned, your opponent may well be doing the same thing from a less than scientific stand point.

For this reason the truly conscious martial artist continues to practice and refine effective street-fighting techniques with equally-trained partners, to understand what may logically follow from one technique on to the next in street-fighting encounters.

The most effective way to set up a practice structure where you can learn what to do in each type of encounter is to allow both your practice opponent and yourself to flow from one technique and on to the next, as it would occur in a street fight. The object of this type of training is, you both continue on with blocking, deflection, grappling and counter-striking techniques until one of you either locks the other one into a hold that he can not recover from, or a controlled strike is delivered that would fully debilitate an opponent on the street.

As we have seen, your opponent is continually moving from one position and technique onto the next. Once your opponent has relocated his physical positioning, you must be consciously willing and effectively able to alter whatever position you are in or whichever self-defense technique you are performing in order to move onto a better and more effective placement, with the ability to more efficiently penetrate his defenses.

Therefore, any defensive technique that involves complicated movements or attacks which require your opponent to remain in one position for more than a second can be ruled out.

Traditional martial arts classroom training generally does not teach you how to deal with this type of movement confrontation. It is true, in many sparring situations, at martial arts schools or tournaments, you have been taught to follow one offensive technique with the next. This kick follows that punch and so on.

This routine, however, is all too pretty The streets are not like that. A person jumps on you and begins to pound, pull, scratch or bite away You must learn to be able to deal effectively with this type of street-fighting situation.

Range Effectiveness

This brings us to the necessity to be "range effective" in all street-

Your opponent is about to punch you (1). By quickly stepping in and hitting him (2), you gain first strike advantage.

fighting encounters. What this means is that if you have to lean or stretch your body out for, say, a punch to reach your opponent, this technique should not be performed. By leaning out like this, you have no doubt exposed your ribs, stomach and groin area to your opponent. Once you have opened your body up like this, the trained street brawler may well have the ability to launch a powerful attack and strike you in any region which you have exposed to him.

This is equally the case with any type of grappling that may take place in a street fight. The performance of whatever disengaging or throwing technique you perform should be able to be performed by your body to such a degree that it does not throw you off balance or open you up for your assailant to have an easy ability to hit or kick at you.

The way to be truly range effective and consciously launch any attack or counterattack at your opponent is to know, through partner practice, just how far you may extend any limb of your body without overly exposing your body to counter-attack potential. Once any appropriate technique is launched, you must be willing and able to quickly stop it and pull it back if your opponent rapidly moves out of the way and repositions himself. If this occurs, you must be able to quickly launch into another attack, which will be more effective in the new range that has been defined.

The final stage to understanding effective street fighting is to never make any motion with your body without directed focus in mind. This is what separates the truly trained martial artist from the brawling street fighter. You must have an intended placement for all of your strikes, blocks and body grabs. Even though we now understand they may need to be realigned, while in motion, continued simulated street-fighting drills will train you to do this effectively and be an efficient self-protector on the ever worsening streets we live on. ■

Scott Shaw is a black belt and writer who lives in Hermosa Beach, California.

24

IKF PRESENTS

DECEMBER 1993
K48745
$3.00 U.S.
$3.50 in Canada
£1.95 DGS

COMPLETE GUIDE TO KICKING & STRETCHING

Muay Thai's Master Toddy

The Logic of Leg Kicks MUAY THAI'S WICKED WEAPON

How to Perform Effective Flying Kicks

Hapkido's Circular Kicks
STRAIGHT TO THE POINT OF DESTRUCTION

Hapkido's Scott Shaw

JON NIELSEN

Speed Up By Slowing Down
The Art of Broken Rhythm Kicking

Plus: Basic & Advanced Stretching Tips from Two Great Champions

CFW ENTERPRISES, INC.
20th Anniversary
1973-1993

0   71896 48745   9

12

25

Hapkido's Circular Kicks –

By Scott Shaw

Photos by Joel Ciniero

Straight to the Point

The Korean martial art of Hapkido, long known for its joint-locking and throwing techniques, has a devastating arsenal of kicks. Hapkido is a confrontational-based martial art system. It does not spend long training sessions developing the ability of tournament point-fighters. The Hapkido kicking theory, therefore, believes that no kick should ever be performed unless it can have the desired result on your opponent, which is generally the ending of your assailant's assault.

Hapkido was first envisioned by its founder, Yong Shul Choi, in the early part of the twentieth century while studying Daito-ryu Aikijujutsu in Japan. He brought the martial art system he developed back to his native country, Korea, where it evolved further and was integrated with the powerful kicking technique indigenous to the Korean peninsula. Therefore, not only does Hapkido possess a veritable array of hand techniques commonly associated with such martial arts as Aikido and Jujitsu, but it has an armory of kicking techniques as well.

Hapkido bases all of its fighting techniques, including its kicks, on circular movements. There are several ways in which the Hapkido practitioner uses its circular theory

> "Hapkido bases all of its kicks on circular movements, first, by allowing the legs to flow in natural patterns. What this means is, the kicking movements are not forced to take an unnatural movement path, as is often the case with the very flamboyant kicks of some of the other martial art systems."

of defense to define its kicking strategy

First of all, Hapkido incorporates its circular format into its kicking techniques by allowing the legs to flow in natural patterns. What this means is, the kicking movements are not forced to take an unnatural movement path, as is often the case with the very flamboyant kicks of some of the other mar-

tial art systems. By allowing the legs to flow in natural patterns, this allows not only the development of additional power to their kicking strikes but aids in its kicks not causing injury to the leg of the practitioner as well.

Hapkido Vs. Tae Kwon Do

To understand Hapkido's circular kicking theory more precisely we can compare it to the the more predominant Korean martial art of Tae Kwon Do. Thus understanding how two martial art styles, developed in the same country, view kicking applications quite differently

There are two specific kicks which will illustrate the difference between the two martial arts quite effectively; they are the crescent kick and the roundhouse kick.

In Tae Kwon Do, the crescent kick is brought straight up and then the strike is performed

with your heel being forcefully brought down onto your opponent's shoulder. Your leg is kept very straight while this kick is being performed. The Tae Kwon Do crescent kick is often referred to, colloquially, as an "Axe" kick.

Hapkido's belief is that this is far too slow of a kicking technique, leaving it easily defended against by the competent opponent. Also, by keeping the kicking leg very straight in this fashion it leaves your knee open to being damaged easily

Hapkido's crescent kick, on the other hand, flows in a circular pattern. It is performed by lifting the leg at the hip level, the knee of the kicking leg then circularly, either in-to-out or out-to-in, circumvents the body, reaching its highest point at approximately your shoulder level. The impact is made with the side of your foot striking across your opponent's face or body By executing the crescent

kick in this fashion, not only is it a very rapid and penetrating technique, the knee remains bent, thus keeping it from being easily injured.

"Hapkido's belief is that even though the trained opponent may indeed see its roundhouse kick coming more readily than modern Tae Kwon Do's redefined roundhouse, it is not important, for the power incurred through this type of continual motion kicking technique will inflict damage to whatever part of the body it impacts on the opponent."

The second kick we can compare between the Korean martial arts of Hapkido and Tae Kwon Do to gain a deeper understanding of the kicking principals of Hapkido is the roundhouse kick.

Modern Tae Kwon Do has redefined the usage of the traditional roundhouse kick by having the kicking leg first move upward, in a linear fashion, until the knee of the kicking leg is located somewhere between the waist and the chest level. The base foot and the hip of the Tae Kwon Do practitioner then pivots, as the kicking foot is turned and snapped to its final target.

Tae Kwon Do's belief is that by performing the roundhouse kick in this fashion, first straight up and then pivoting it to the side, it is less vulnerable to blocks. Though this may indeed be the case, thus making the kick effective in Tae Kwon Do tournaments, it decreases its power immensely, making it virtually completely ineffective for altercations on the street.

The modern Tae Kwon Do roundhouse kick is also slowed down greatly; as the kicking leg must first

28

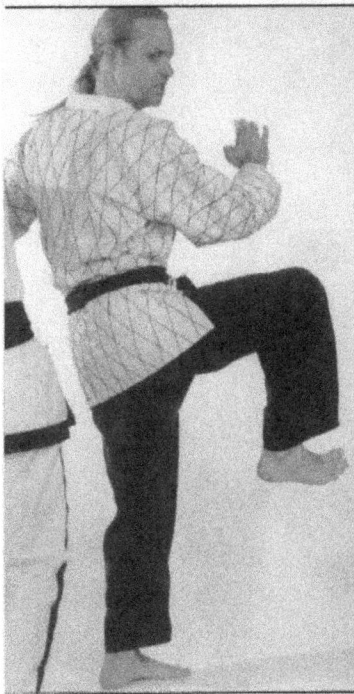

Your opponent attempts a straight punch at you. You block it with a crescent kick (1 & 2). You then deliver a spinning back crescent kick to his head, debilitating him (3, 4 & 5).

be projected in one motion, upwards, and then changed to the side motion of the traditional roundhouse. By performing a roundhouse kick in this fashion it becomes much slower to execute and the majority of its power is lost. For these reasons it is no longer a truly effective kicking technique except for point-scoring tournaments.

Hapkido's circular roundhouse is executed in a traditional fashion by bringing the kicking leg up, in a motion directed at the target in a rapid continuous motion. The base foot pivots, while the striking leg develops speed and power from the continual motion of the momentum gained from the kicking leg moving in one continuous pattern to the striking point. As the foot approaches its target it is powerfully snapped out from the knee adding additional power to the strike of Hapkido's traditional roundhouse.

29

You are engaged in a confrontational situation (1). Your opponent moves towards you. You hook kick him at knee level (2) and immediately continue through with a hook kick to his head (3 & 4).

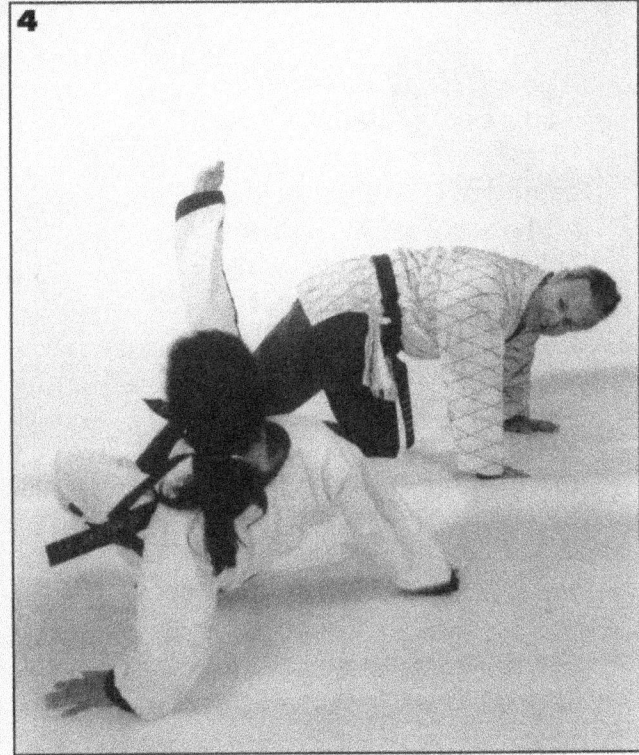

Your opponent comes at you. Before he has the chance to make the first move, you perform a spinning sweep kick(1 & 2), sending him to the ground (3 & 4).

Hapkido's belief is that even though the trained opponent may indeed see this type of roundhouse kick coming more readily than modern Tae Kwon Do's redefined roundhouse, it is not important, for the power incurred through this type of continual motion kicking technique will inflict damage to whatever part of the body it impacts on the opponent.

The Power of Hapkido Kicks

The power of the Hapkido kick is gained from the moment it is launched and the leg is lifted from the ground. This is the reason such kicks as the crescent and the roundhouse are so powerful. The power is instigated by the muscles in the leg at the point the kick has begun, then momentum force is added and finally it is snapped into final strike positioning just at the moment of impact.

> **"Though Hapkido bases its kicks on circular motion, Hapkido's kicks are performed in a straight-to-the-target fashion. In Hapkido kicking, no unnecessary leg movement is ever performed. Thus, all Hapkido kicking techniques are limited to ones that have the potential of powerfully connecting with your opponent."**

Hapkido is a confrontational-based martial art system. It does not spend long training sessions developing the ability of tournament point-fighters. The Hapkido kicking theory, therefore, believes that no kick should ever be performed unless it can have the desired result on your opponent, which is generally the ending of your assailant's assault.

Though Hapkido bases its kicks on circular motion, Hapkido's kicks are performed in a straight-to-the-target fashion. In Hapkido kicking, no unnecessary leg movement is ever performed. You do not perform kicks at your opponent, just to educate him to the fact that you may indeed be able to execute a pretty kick. Though that is an exaggerated example, it is a quite common occurrence.

In a confrontational situation, you also do not fake with one kicking technique in the hopes of continuing through with another offense. If you attempt to fake an opponent in this fashion you are leaving yourself vulnerable to a quick and unperceived counterstrike from a trained adversary Thus, all kicking techniques are limited to ones that have the potential of powerfully connecting with your opponent.

Though Hapkido applies circular theory to its kicks, this does not mean that it does not use straight kicking techniques such as the front kick, side kick and the various variations which they entail. Hapkido does view the spectrum of martial arts in circular theory; yet, by doing so it does not alienate the usefulness of any other appropriate fighting techniques, be they seemingly circular or straight.

Circular Vs. Linear and Vice Versa

To place this into the realm of a more clearly understood and usable application, what this means is that a defensive circular technique, such as a roundhouse or spinning heel kick, has a greater ability of pivoting around and rapidly striking your opponent who launches a straight technique — such as a side kick at you — than does one have by going toe-to-toe and meeting a straight-on technique with another straight technique.

This is also the case with the ability a straight technique, such as a front kick, has in intercepting and halting the onslaught of a circular offense such as a roundhouse kick. By working within this theory, of meeting a straight technique with a circular one and vice versa, you have the ability of easily penetrating and defeating your opponent's offensive movements.

> **"An additional element to Hapkido's circular theory is its 'Periphery of Defense.' To understand this, envision a circle extending around your body approximately three feet in diameter. This is your range of offense and defense. Whenever you encounter a confrontational situation and your opponent enters this range, this is when you take action."**

Another key point of Hapkido's circular-kicking theory involves the continuum of motion of flowing from one defensive or offensive technique directly onto the next. This means that once you have blocked a punch you immediately flow through with a debilitating kick to your opponent. Or, once you have launched and connected a strike to your opponent you immediately deliver another one to seal his fate. By approaching martial arts in this way the Hapkido practitioner leaves his opponent no time to launch further assaults on his body

This continual motion is viewed by the Hapkido practitioner as an encompassing circular pattern, moving continually from one martial application immediately onto the next

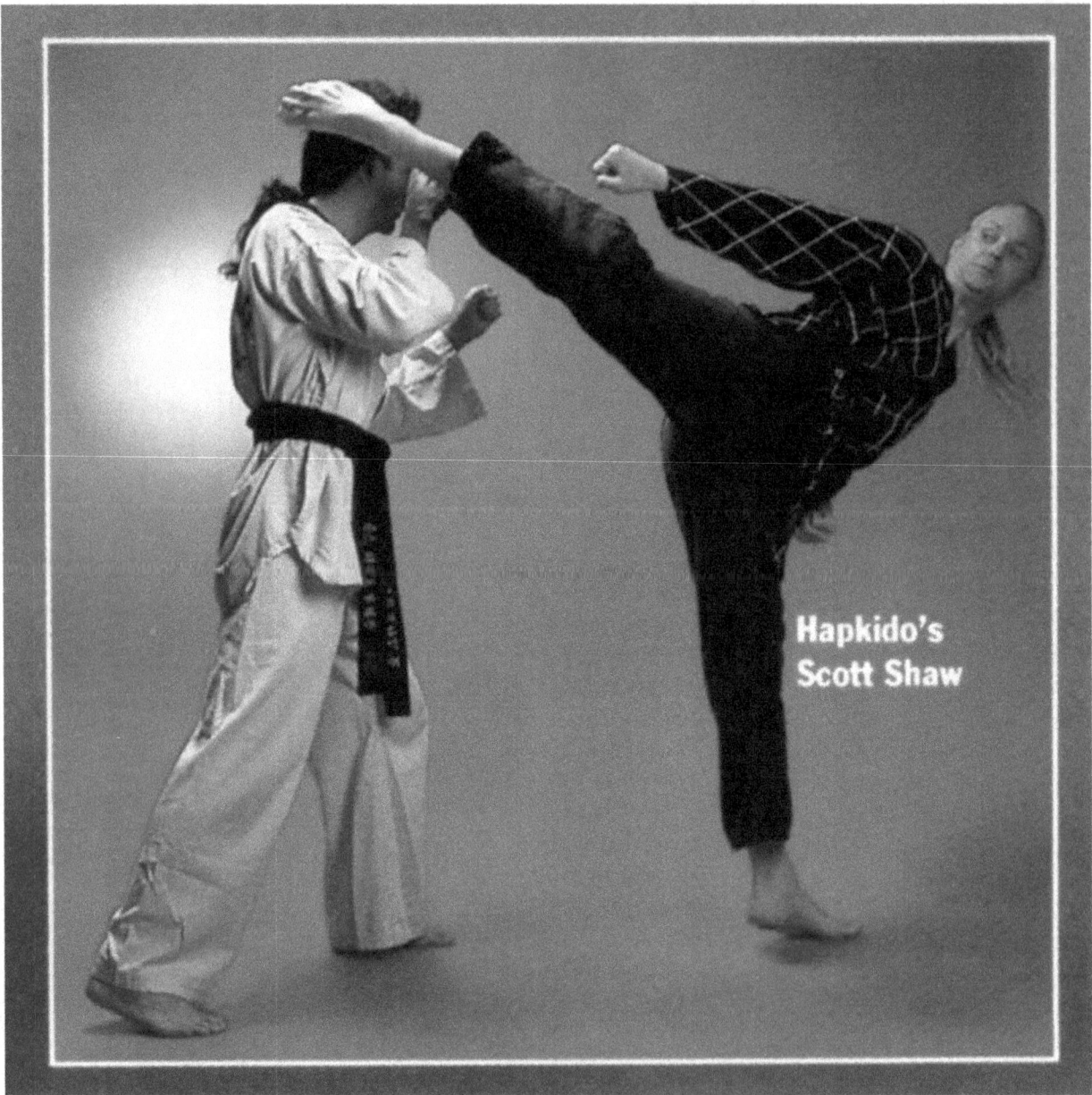

Hapkido's
Scott Shaw

most appropriate technique. Hapkido kicking theory works on the same basis of this continuing circular motion; from one kicking application to the next until the opponent is defeated. To this end, Hapkido's circular kicking technique ideally flows easily from one onto the next. A spinning heel kick easily follows a roundhouse kick. A spinning back crescent kick effortlessly follows a forward crescent kick, and so on.

The circular kicking patterns a Hapkido fighter follows allows one to flow evenly and continuously from one fighting technique onto the next. For this reason all of your kicks should be launched to follow one another quickly and easily

One of the additional elements of the martial philosophy of Hapkido is, "Total penetration of an opponent's offenses and defenses." To this end, Hapkido achieves this goal with the use of powerfully well-trained legs. The combination of penetrating the opponent's movements with its kicks and the continual flowing circular techniques allows Hapkido to be one of the most truly effective martial art forms.

Hapkido's "Periphery of Defense"

An additional element to Hapkido's circular theory is its "Periphery of Defense." To understand this, envision a circle extending around your body approximately three feet in diameter. This is your range of offense and defense. Whenever you encounter a confrontational situation and your opponent enters this range, this is when you take action. Of course, this range moves with your body as you move.

The reason this approximate three-feet limit is set around you is that this keeps you from overextending your

Your opponent attempts to straight punch you. You block it (1 & 2) and immedately pivot into a spinning heel kick to his head (3, 4 & 5).

applicable kick and body motions, be they offensive or defensive. If your opponent is beyond this range, to take defensive action is generally unnecessary, as your opponent is too far away from you to cause harm.

It is far better to allow him to enter into this range, thus, by stabilizing your positioning you will maintain the advantage. From an offensive stand point, by attempting to make your techniques reach out of this area to engage your opponent, you may well overextend yourself or throw yourself off-balance, thus giving him the advantage.

Though certain kicking techniques are obviously designed to reach out at a distance, such as the stepping side kick, the jumping side kick and so on, in a one-to-one confrontational situation where your opponent has no weapon, the Hapkido practitioner believes that by going to the opponent you give them the advantage of remaining stable while you are traveling. For this reason, it is again better to let them move to you.

Thus, the way Hapkido's approximate three-foot circle or periphery of defense further is further involved and aids in your kicking strategy, is that, by staying firm in your original positioning and allowing your opponent to come to you, the moment he enters your circle he can easily be struck by a kick as he recklessly charges at you.

With basic understanding of the principals behind the use of the kicking techniques of Hapkido, we now have the more clearly perceived ability to make every offense a truly effective martial arts technique. ☁

Scott Shaw is a Hermosa Beach, California-based actor writer and Hapkido black belt.

Closing the Gap

Hapkido-Style

Confrontations do not always begin nose-to-nose with your opponent. Often, especially in random street encounters, either your opponent will rush in at you from a distance or you will need to rapidly close the gap yourself, before he has the ability to use that distance to his own advantage. Here's how to move from long to short range, Hapkido-style.

By Scott Shaw

Distance, between your adversary and you, does not need to be your enemy. As an evolving martial artist you can learn how to effectively close any gap between you and your opponent. You can not only strike him first, but as the Korean martial art of Hapkido teaches, continue forward with effective defensive and offensive techniques which will disable your opponent and disallow him to continue forward with additional attacks on you.

In the art of distance fighting, you need to, first of all, keep in mind that the streets are not a sanctioned sparring match where you can step back and allow a referee to award you a point after each successful attack. You need to defend yourself and strike decisively, in order that your battle will not end up on the ground in a haphazard grappling match, which is to no one's advantage

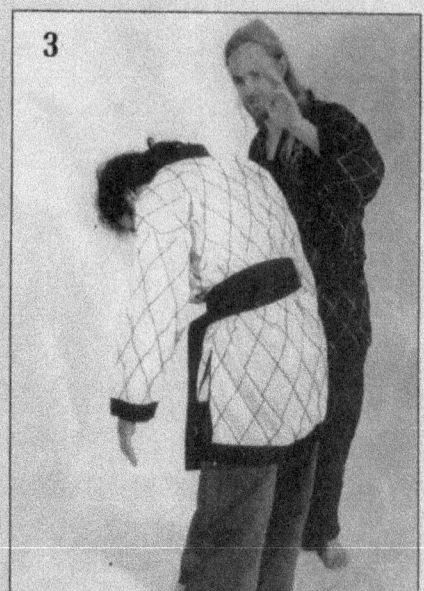

You rapidly drive in at your opponent, under his guard, with an extended front kick. Immediately upon completion of the kick, you grab his neck, locking it. You throw him to the ground.

There are two issues you need to study to come to understand how to successfully deal with an opponent at a distance. The first of which is how to rapidly penetrate his defenses and make the initial strike. The second is how to successfully defend against an adversary who is attacking you from a distance.

Modify Your Front Kick

To examine this from a scientific standpoint, when you view your opponent (at a distance) he is obviously awaiting your attack. Generally, he will be standing in a ready fighting position, with his fists at chest level. What you can observe by studying his stance, is his lower extremities are open for attack.

To launch a successful attack, and beat the your opponent's possible blocking-arm counters, you need to move in quickly and powerfully. One of the best ways to achieve this, is to instantly extend a front kick to your opponent's groin or solar plexus.

Many traditional martial artists extend

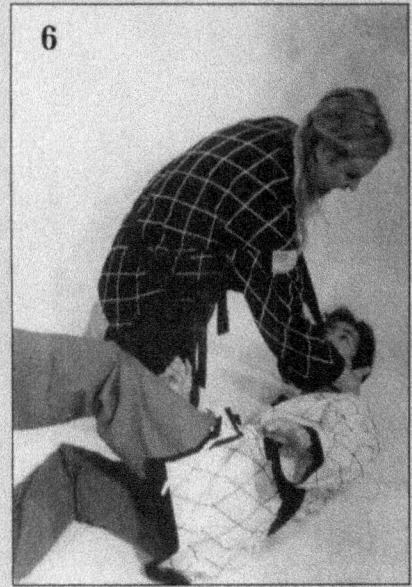

their front kicks very obviously from their hip. When the front kick is delivered in traditional fashion, it is snapped out and up. This type of traditional front kick is not an effective form of self-defense, especially when your opponent is at any distance from you. This is because, when the front kick is performed in the traditional manner, it has no ability to achieve distance and its energy is expended in upward movement. Your opponent can simply lean back away from it and the attack will miss.

The more effective front kick, especially when there is a need to cover distance, is to not focus the kick in an upward fashion, but to extend it from your rear leg outwards in the direction of your opponent. By performing the front kick in this fashion, you not only can gain enormous distance with it, due to the fact that the kicks own momentum drives you deeply forward, but it also will penetrate under your opponent's traditional fighting stance.

Once you have made initial contact with

You penetrate your opponent's defenses with a stepping ax kick. Once you have made contact with his shoulder you reverse knife hand strike his neck. You continue through, throwing him to the ground over your hip.

this front kick and, hopefully, stunned your opponent to a degree, Hapkido teaches that you must instantaneously continue forward with additional disabling techniques to your opponent. By fighting in this fashion, your opponent does not have the opportunity to successfully secondarily counterstrike at you.

The Neck as a Target

In Hapkido, we learn the neck is one of the most exposed and disabling targets on the human body. By controlling your opponent's neck, you dominate virtually any movement he may make. To this end, once your front kick has penetrated your opponent's initial defenses, you can easily reach in and make a two-handed grab at your opponent's head, in order to control his neck. You should grab your opponent with one hand under his chin and jaw to the front and your other hand should take control of the back of his head, to the rear.

Once you have gained this hold, simply by arching and twisting his neck, you lock

it into place, and will have gained virtually total control over your opponent. From here, by simply pivoting your body, you can send him effortlessly to the ground.

The Stepping Ax Kick

A secondary offensive technique which is effectively launched at your opponent is to perform a stepping ax kick to his shoulder. The stepping ax kick not only quickly covers much distance, but its impact is devastating to your opponent. As your opponent will no doubt be waiting in a fighting position, the stepping ax kick easily penetrates his defenses by going over them, this time, instead of under them.

The stepping ax kick is effectively performed by rapidly placing your rear leg behind your forward leg, thus giving you added distance. As this movement is performed, you will raise your forward leg straight up. Once you have achieved your desired location, close to your opponent, you powerfully bring your ax kick down

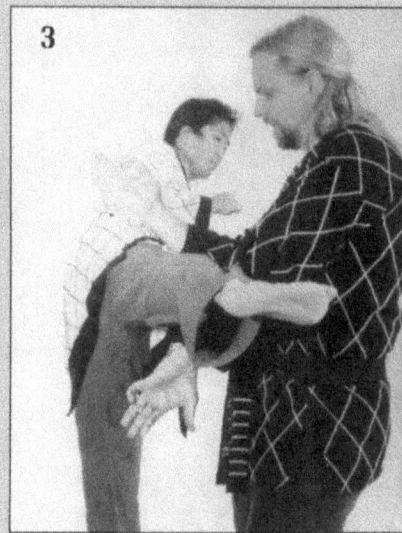

Your opponent charges at you with a stepping side kick. You side step and deflect the kick. Immediately, you strike at your opponent's neck. Then, by lifting his leg up, you throw him to the ground.

onto his shoulder.

Though the stepping ax kick, itself, is a very powerful kicking technique, you should always continue forward with additional techniques, until your opponent is on the ground and you are sure he will cause no further risk to your safety.

Once you have successfully performed your stepping ax kick, your opponent's neck will again be exposed to additional offensive techniques. This time, by first powerfully striking him to his throat with a reverse knife-hand blow, you can then continue forward by leaving your arm in place at his neck level and effortless throw him over your hip to the ground.

As we have seen, closing the distance between your adversary and yourself is not difficult, when executed properly. The important thing to remember is one technique is rarely enough to emerge victorious from a confrontation, therefore, additional techniques to seal your opponent's fate should always be performed.

As there are no guarantees you will have the ability to be the first to move on your opponent, we must also study effective methods to defend against your opponent's oncoming assault at you from a distance.

When Your Opponent Closes the Gap

The stepping side kick is no doubt one of the universally most powerful techniques in any martial artist's arsenal. It is, as well, a very good method to close the distance on your opponent. Knowing this, what happens if your opponent launches this attack technique at you?

The stepping side kick, by its very design, is very linear. It is performed by plac-

ing your rear leg behind your front leg and rapidly extending your front leg in side-kick fashion. As powerful as this kicking technique is, its linear nature is its weakness, which allows it to be defended against.

Your opponent attempts to perform a stepping side kick at you. You slide your body to one side, the impact of the kick thereby misses its target on your body. While

The stepping ax kick not only quickly covers much distance, but its impact is devastating to your opponent. As your opponent will no doubt be waiting in a fighting position, the stepping ax kick easily penetrates his defenses by going over them, this time, instead of under them.

side-stepping the kick, you should be deflecting it, as well, with a cross arm block. The need for this added deflection arises because, by deflecting the kick, you momentarily take control over your opponent's kicking leg and thereby keep him from rapidly grounding it and perhaps backfisting you.

Once you have side-stepped and deflected the stepping side kick, the next course of action you should take is to powerfully knife-hand strike your opponent to his face or neck. Once your strike has made contact, you should rapidly lift his kicking leg up and over himself, with the arm you have left in position to maintain control over his movements.

By performing these movements virtually simultaneously, you not only gain first strike on your opponent, but you send him to the ground as well, where you can continue forward with additional counterattacks as necessary.

Jumping Side Kick

Another very effective distance gainer is the jumping side kick. This kick is launched by stepping your rear leg in front of your forward leg, jumping off of it, and side kicking your opponent. Though this kick is very distance-penetrating and powerful, it has the same flaw as the stepping side kick: its linear nature. Additionally, the jumping side kick is more pronounced and slower than the stepping side kick.

Therefore, if your opponent attempts to attack you with it, your initial defense it to side step.

As you remove yourself from the path of the jumping side kick, you should simultaneously straight punch your opponent to his

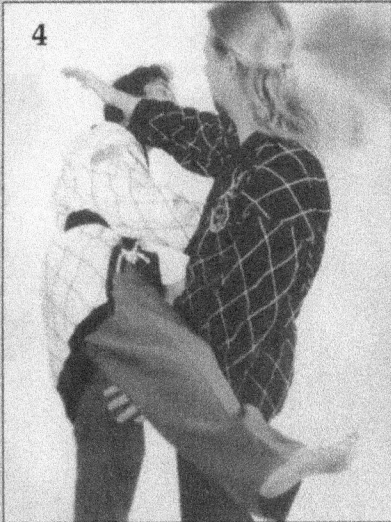

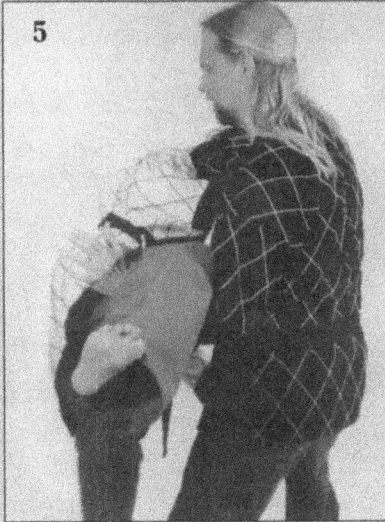

There are two issues you need to study to come to understand how to successfully deal with an opponent at a distance. The first of which is how to rapidly penetrate his defenses and make the initial strike. The second is how to successfully defend against an adversary who is attacking you from a distance.

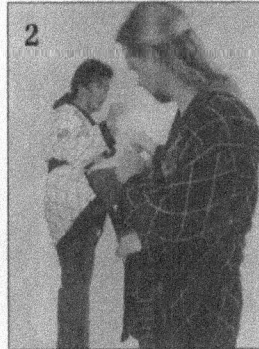

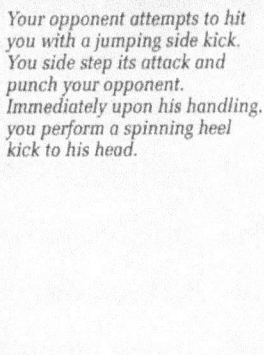

Your opponent attempts to hit you with a jumping side kick. You side step its attack and punch your opponent. Immediately upon his handling, you perform a spinning heel kick to his head.

midsection or his face. As the jumping side kick is a momentum-driven kick, your opponent does not have the ability to effectively stop it once it is launched. As well, once this kick is in progress and you have side-stepped it, your opponent is left open for this effective counterpunch.

Since your straight punch may not have a completely debilitating effect on your opponent, you must, as in all cases, immediately follow it up with additional defensive techniques. Because your opponent will be slightly off balance, due to his kick missing and your punching him, you can easily follow up with an additional punch to the back of his head or a powerful kick, such as a spinning heel kick, to his face.

Conclusion

As you have come to understand, distance between you and your opponent does not have to be a disadvantage. You can either launch the first attack, closing the distance, or if your opponent is, "first-out-of-the-gate" you can effectively defend against his attack.

By making distance fighting a science and by studying its elements, you can learn how to effectively use it to your advantage.
■

Scott Shaw is a Hapkido black belt, a writer and actor from Hermosa Beach, California. He has just launched a series of Hapkido instructional videotapes for Unique Videos (see ad in this issue).

ECONOMY

OF MOTION

The Offense

of Defense

By Dr. Scott Shaw, PhD

n any physical confrontation there is one, and only one, ultimate goal in mind: survival, by the most rapid means possible. What this entails is to deliver the first blow, not allowing your opponent to have that first-strike advantage. This is accomplished by becoming aware of, and utilizing, the shortest distance between two points; namely: your fist, foot, elbow, or knee, and the targeted area on your opponent. In other words, defense that is offense. This concept has come to be popularly known as "economy of motion."

Conventional Training

As martial artists, we are all trained how to block, where best to impact our strikes, and how to get out of the way of oncoming assaults. Generally, the traditional martial arts choose to take a lengthy, round about way to achieve this. Conventional training teaches one to step back, block, and then counter With today's sophisticated fighters, this extended method of self defense is no longer a viable means of protection.

As we view what economy of motion entails, its basic principle is to lessen the amount of physical movement and thereby speed up the strike to an opponent. Within this framework, every strike, block, or movement must have an absolute necessity and a destined end goal, or there is no purpose in performing it. The most obvious example

The basic principle of economy of motion is to lessen the amount of physical movement and thereby speed up the strike to an opponent.

45

A roundhouse kick is launched by your opponent. A punch to the leg, stops its advance. While the opponent is sent back by its force, a back-fist is delivered to the face.

of this is why must, say, a roundhouse kick be blocked and then a counter assault launched when it is far more expedient to simply block the oncoming kick with a punch to the opponent's leg. Thereby, not only have you delivered the first blow, but you have possibly injured the opponent's leg, as well. And, in doing so you have begun your road to victory over the assailant.

Theories of Defense

All defensive techniques must be actually offensive. It is far better to strike than to block. Why? Because, how many times in training have you blocked a technique and in doing so been bruised or injured? As all martial artists know, the impact of any kick, punch, or strike has the ability to damage a person, whether intentional or not. It is for this reason that those who practice economy of motion meet an on coming attack with a strike instead of a possibly damaging block.

Step out of the way of a technique rather than encounter it. Duck, bob, weave, move back, then immediately strike a return blow.

You can never anticipate or know what an opponent may have in mind. It is for this reason that you must never waste

It is far better to strike than to block.

time with remedial defensive techniques. Do not block a technique with the hopes of following through with a counter attack. A trained fighter may only be performing a specific technique as a ploy and may actually plan to strike with something else once your retreating movement has been initiated. Thus, it is better to step inside the oncoming technique and

launch a punch or kick and circumvent the opponent's attack.

Theories of Offense

A straight ahead assault is far faster, and much harder to block or deflect than a circular technique. It is for this reason that a punch should be launched straight ahead, from the elbow and not thrown circularly, roundhouse style, from the shoulder This way it will go inside any techniques the adversary is attempting to do.

The hands are closer to an opponents head than are the feet; use them. The head is the bodily region where the most nonpermanent damage can be inflicted upon an assailant. By aiming here, one can often times leave the scene immediately after the first strike.

In traditional martial arts sparring matches, kicking techniques such as a roundhouse kick or a spinning heel kick are launched towards an opponent's head. This is fine, in a friendly atmosphere. On the streets, it is a far different story. It takes too

The opponent attempts a back-fist. Quickly, stepping inside of its range a straight-punch is launched and hits the opponent's face.

A straight-punch is attempted by the opponent. By quickly stepping inside of it and launching your own straight-punch, you are not struck by the blow but your opponent is.

The opponent attempts to perform a back or spinning heel kick. It is intercepted by a front kick to the butt and their body is shoved away. A punch then strikes the back of the head.

long for that type of technique to reach the opponent's head and there are too many ways to block it. Once again, a straight front kicking technique is far faster and more difficult to avoid.

There is no way of knowing how competent a fighter your opponent may be. It is for this reason that one should always meet any aggression with a devastating blow. Perform every technique with devastation of the opponent in mind. This may sound heartless, but, how many times has a warrior shown sympathy to an opponent, only to be taken advantage of when the adversary has regained their standing?

Once you start a move, you are committed. Never hesitate or re-think your movement while it is in motion. By not performing it instantaneously, your opponent may take advantage of this momentary lapse of advance and use this time against you.

There are two basic problems which the majority of martial artists encounter, when they are either unwittingly accosted by a street fighter, or while sparring a very competent fighter from a different style in the ring; they are: one, the martial artists choose to use techniques which they have not fully comprehended.

It is what all those who understand economy of motion avoid at all cost. Never attempt a technique you have not fully

Never attempt a technique you have not fully mastered!

mastered! Use simplicity, it is a warrior's best friend. It is better to stay simple than to try to impress and lose the bout.

The second biggest problem a martial artist encounters in defense is to believe that his own specific school of martial arts holds no equals, and then place it up against another style and be devastated by the opponent. This is a very common occurrence with those martial artists who encounter, say, a trained boxer, kickboxer, or a avid street fighter; someone whose techniques are random and completely different. The only reason this devastation occurs is that one allows the ego and illusion that one style is superior to all others to control him. It is essential in today's shrinking world to view, study, and understand all fighting styles, even if you don't agree with them or approve of them.

A good method to overcome the aforementioned problem is, while training or sparring in your school, throw the rules out the window and let what happens happen.

In accordance with this, the first step to understand the absolute theory of economy of motion is to lose all those techniques, which, though they may be impressive to perform, have no real value in confrontational situations. It is very common that martial arts schools teach numerous 'self defense' techniques that just will not work in actually fight situa-

The opponent performs a spinning crescent kick. By leaning your body back and out of the way, the kick misses. Immediately, an inside front kick strikes the opponent in the face.

tions. The best way to find these out is to put them to the test while still at the school. See if they really block the punch, break the hold, or throw the opponent.

Developing Economy of Motion

The first step in developing the usage of economy of motion is to define your own abilities and what you have trained your mind to believe is the appropriate reaction to any given action. Let's investigate what works, what does not, and why. First of all if you have a training partner you can do this with, great; if not, for now, just perform it with an imaginary partner.

Stand in a slight traditional horse stance, your opponent in front of you. If he were to punch or kick at you, what would you need to do to get out of the way of that assault? Yes, it would take considerable movement to avoid that attack. Try this same scenario in a back or front stance. Are your reactions slowed down as well? Yes. This is why stances like this are never used when dealing with economy of motion; the movement in or out is too time consuming.

Stand in a traditional fighting stance, whatever your style teaches or you feel is correct. Your opponent launches various assaults at you. What is your immediate reaction to them? Would it be to step out of the way, to block, to strike, or kick? Which ones actually perform the goal of expedient victory over your opponent?

Now, let's try something else. Stand with your side facing the opponent, lift your arms as if you were boxing, fists closed (always keep your hands in fist position, it saves them from being easily broken). Let your knees be loose. Stand light on your feet, as if dancing. Now, an opponent attacks. How much actual space would they have to frontally strike at your body? Not much, right? Can you easily move out of the way and back in, to attack? Yes.

Let's take this a step further, allow them to launch various attacks and instead of simply moving out of the way or blocking, defend with a purpose; find ways to move inside on their kicks or punches with your own counter attacks and strike.

Economy of motion teaches one to use the closest component to the assailant and strike with it; be it your fist, leg, elbow, or whatever To do this at the most rapid rate possible allows first strike capabilities and keeps one from unnecessarily using energy by having to dodge or block the attack of the opponent. It is for this reason that one should fight with their lead arm and leg forward.

An example of the usefulness of this is quite simple; your opponent attempts to kick or punch, use the lead leg in a front or side kick fashion, kick to the stomach region and the attack has been halted and again you have gained, first strike.

As time has progressed and as the various fighting styles from around the world have come to a better understanding of one another, today's insightful martial artists have taken techniques from each style and integrated the best of all forms of defense and offense into their own personal adaption. What has been born, especially in America, is a styling down of the traditional martial arts and a birth of an eclectic warfare that incorporated, at it's heart, the principle of economy of motion.

No Holds Barred — Self-Defense for the Street

Where rules don't count

By Scott Shaw

As our streets have become increasingly unsafe and random acts of violence have seemingly become the norm, it has become an absolute need rather than just a passing interest that all of us; women and men alike, must understand how to quickly and effectively protect ourselves against any would be assailant. Personal self defense is often passed over to the belief that it, "Will not happen to me." This is the biggest misconception an individual can hold. Time and time again it has been proven that one must be prepared at all time, for an unexpected confrontational situation.

The second biggest mistake people make in the realms of erroneous self-defense, is that they believe the weapon they may carry be it mace, a stun gun a knife, or even a gun, will be all they need to protect themselves. Of course, these objects may prevent certain attacks or fend off others. But, what if the weapon is taken away from you in the heat of the confrontation by a well schooled street fighter? Then, not only does the attacker have the weapon, but it can be used against you as well. For these reasons and the worsening conditions of society you must prepare yourself for any possible altercation.

The first and most obvious form of self-defense for the street is to leave the situation immediately run if necessary If this is not possible, give up

51

Your opponent grabs a hold of your arm. You locate where his thumbs are. Then, with the aid of your other hand grabbing a hold of your clasped arm you pull upwards against his thumbs; instantly releasing his grip. You continue through with an elbow strike to his jaw.

"A fight is won or lost in the first few movements and generally the first strike is what sets the stage for who wins the confrontation."

your money watch, or car There is nothing degrading about this, as no material object is worth any unpredictable results from a confrontation with a street assailant. If all else fails and you must save your body or your life, then concise street self defense must be put into play

To train in essential self defense, you need not study for hours every day at the Dojo, or perform Kata for years under the lineage of some Great Grand Master from Asia. What it does take is some simple, basic understanding of the human body and when and where to strike if you are accosted by an individual with less than sociable behavior in mind.

To begin our development of essential self defense we must first and foremost come to the understanding that no confrontation is ever won by a long exchange of punches, as is the case in the movies. A fight is won or lost in the first few movements and generally the first strike is what sets the stage for who wins the confrontation.

THE MYTH OF GROIN STRIKES

What then, is the first strike focal point in relation to self defense? Often time people believe a strike to a male's groin will disable him. To a certain degree this is true. In practice, however the ability to achieve a very focused and powerful strike, either with the hand, knee, or foot, to this region is limited by many things, including articles of clothing and the opponent's movement.

Furthermore, a missed strike to this groin region will only anger your attacker more and give him the advantage of striking at you Even if one successfully strikes an attacker in the groin, this will only debilitate him for a moment. Thus, the groin is a viable preliminary target, but do not base your entire self-defense strategy on it.

EFFECTIVE FIRST STRIKES

If an adversary comes at you; the two most expedient first strike zones to end the assault quickly and the ones that take the least amount of

practice are either a foot strike to the opponent's knee or a palm strike under his nose. These two strikes each have their own individual advantages. To use them effectively however they must be correctly understood.

A strike to the opponent's knee is effective whether they accost you frontally or come at you and grab from behind. Though the strike itself is obviously performed a bit differently for each position, the technique is basically the same.

When you strike at an opponent's knee, a simple kick is not enough. Though this may cause minor injury to them, it will not necessarily nullify the attack. The correct technique to successfully strike at the opponent's knee is to powerfully strike your foot into either just at the top of the assailant's knee, or even with it and then, once this initial impact has been made, continue through with a powerful push; delivering all the energy, momentum, and weight of your entire body This technique will instantly debilitate him and his attack will cease.

For frontal attacks there is no better or more direct counter assault than to strike the opponent under his nose with the palm of your hand. To perform this technique most effectively the fingers are bent, causing the base of the palm of your hand to protrude and tighten. The strike is executed with this strengthened base of the palm striking just under the opponent's nose. The force of this impact is geared in an upward motion similar to that of an uppercut punch. Of course, all caution must be used in this technique, whenever it is not meant to be delivered as a death blow When the assailant has no regard for your life, it may however, be the necessary counter attack.

The less fatal application of this strike is to deliver it in the same manner, using the palm hand strike, but the impact point would be across the bridge of your opponent's nose and not upwards and under it, as discussed in the last technique.

Body grabs are, of course, a very common occurrence in street orientated confrontational situations. The best defense at these times is to not allow the adversary to grab a hold of you in the first place. This may sound simplistic but it is much easier to fend off the opponent before they take hold of you than it is once they have taken a strong grip.

To effectively move from an oncoming grab, (provided you see it coming), simply involves rapidly getting out of the way of its reach. By doing this, it has allowed you time to move from the aggressor's attack before it can take hold. Thus, you now have the time to retreat, yell for help, or counter attack.

If an assailant has taken hold of you, however, there are some basic techniques that will allow you to free yourself easily Often times, in a street altercation, one is grabbed by the arm. To get away from this type of arm holding technique, all you need to do is notice where the opponent's thumb is, in relation to where he has grabbed onto your arm or wrist and pull back against it. Due to the design inherent in the human body the opponent's thumb does not have the ability to

uninterruptedly hold your limb, once you know how to disengage it.

A simple experiment anyone can try at home, allowing you to come to a better understanding of this point, is, allow someone to grasp your wrist or arm. You can forcefully yank and pull in the direction of the aggressor's fingers all you want, the only way you will be able to free yourself by attempting to get away from his grip in this manner would be from an act of sheer force. Now try viewing the location of your opponent's thumb and pulling upwards away from it. You will instantly see how easy it is to break your opponent's hold.

If your adversary is extremely strong, it may be necessary to grab a hold of your own hand or wrist to aid you in pulling upwards against his thumb. None the less, freeing yourself in this manner is virtually universally effective.

DEFENDING AGAINST A GRAB

What happens, though, when an opponent has forcefully taken hold of another part of your body? Perhaps he has jumped on you and gotten you in a head lock. The key thing to remember when a situation like this takes place in a street confrontation, is to remain calm and view the weak points of your opponent's grasp.

You must remember to disengage any firm hold on your body: as quickly, easily and effortlessly as possible. Randomly, wrestling with the opponent while attempting to free yourself, is never a good idea. By wrestling, not only do you quickly exhaust your energies but your opponent, due to his superior placement, can easily continually strike you, thus, injuring you while you are attempting to free yourself. Therefore, even in this heat of confrontation, you must quickly analyze your situation and follow the proceeding basic format of freeing yourself.

First of all, the moment the attacker

"If an assailant has taken hold of you, however, there are some basic techniques that will allow you to free yourself easily."

Your opponent wields a knife at you. You deflect it and push it in tight to his body. Instantly, you strike him to his face.

has grabbed you, he is at his weakest point. The longer his hold remains the stronger it will get. Thus, to rapidly free yourself your initial counter defense is to strike your opponent. This hit must be directed at the most debilitating location easily accessible to you. This may be his eyes, nose, temple, or groin, depending on your current location. This hit will not only possibly injure your opponent, but its impact will startle him long enough for him to loosen his hold on you, thus you can move forward with further defensive applications.

A second key point to remember once you have been forcefully

Your opponent holds you in a two handed forward choke hold (1). By bringing your arm up and over his arms, in a powerful motion (2), while slightly pivoting your body, his hold is broken (3). You then, immediately, perform an elbow strike to his face (4).

> **"To rapidly free yourself, your initial counter defense is to strike your opponent."**

An assailant puts a gun to your back. You rapidly pivot around, moving the gun from a range where it can shoot you. You palm strike him under his nose.

grabbed by your opponent, is to make no counter attacking move that will not have at least somewhat of a debilitating effect on him. What this means is that every move to dislocate his hold on you must include a strike. If you are planning to shove him off of you by his neck, do not just put your hand there and push, make your hand into a striking tool and hit his neck as your hand moves into it positioning. Or if you are going to manipulate his elbows to free yourself from a forward hold; strike at them, do not just attempt to move them out of the way

By using this type of striking/disengaging technique whenever and wherever you send any part of your body to meet your opponent's body you will have a cumulative effect on him, thus aiding you in your overall victory in the confrontation.

When freeing yourself from your opponent's grasp, the next step is to rapidly analyze what part of your opponent's body you can most effectively use to manipulate his energy against himself thus causing him to release his grip on you. The two most common locations that are most effective; causing pain to your opponent by forcing manipulation of his body are: one, pulling his hair back, thus locking his neck and two, a strike, then continuing through with further pushing to his neck, in the direction you are planning to send him to the ground.

Once you have made your initial strikes and counter-grabbed your opponent, you must immediately continue through disengaging your adversary's hold on you. To fully disengage his hold you must throw him free from your body in the most natural movement possible, while not allowing him to cling onto you and thus, possibly taking you down with him to the ground

For example, if he has grabbed you, in the previously mentioned head lock, once you have initially struck him, perhaps to the groin with a reverse knife hand, you would instantly grab him by the back of his hair and pull his head back. You would then, while striking to the back of his knee, lift his leg off the ground thus knocking him off balance. Then by both pulling his hair back, while continuing through with a knee lift, you would forcefully throw him backwards to the ground where you would continue through with an additional counter strike to assure he will not come at you again.

If an adversary has grabbed a hold of your lapels or shirt, as is common in the instigation of street fights; similarly by simultaneously grabbing him by the back of his hair twisting it, and forcing his head to one side, thus locking his neck. Then by immediately striking him with a knife hand to his neck, you can easily disengage his hold, as you guide your opponent forcefully to the ground

Though these last two defensive techniques involve the forcible disen-

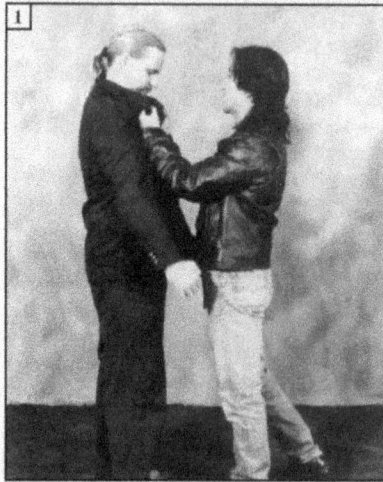

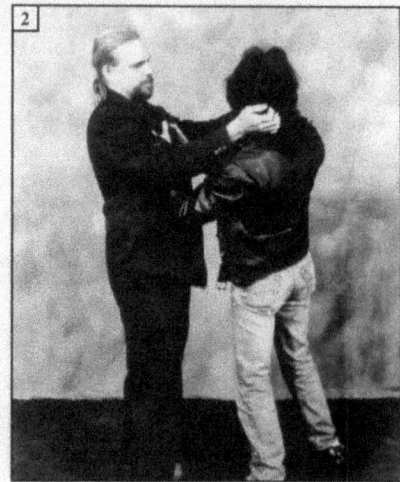

Your lapels are held forcefully by your adversary (1). By grabbing the back of his hair and arching his neck, you lock him into position (2). Then, with the aid of a knife hand to his throat (3), you throw him to the ground (4).

By allowing any opponent's grasp on you to remain in place for any length of time only lessens your chances of eventual victory.

gaging of your opponent's grasp on you, it is very important to realize that in any altercation your ultimate safety is foremost By allowing any opponent's grasp on you to remain in place for any length of time only lessens your chances of eventual victory

With this is mind if an opponent grabs you with a two hand forward choke hold it is quite easily disengaged by simply powerfully bringing your arm up and over his choking arms and striking across them in an angular somewhat downward motion. Instantly his choke hold is released. Now that you have disconnected his hold you must immediately come back, quite effortlessly with an elbow strike to your opponent's head. For without instantly counter striking him he will no doubt come back and unleash a secondary attack.

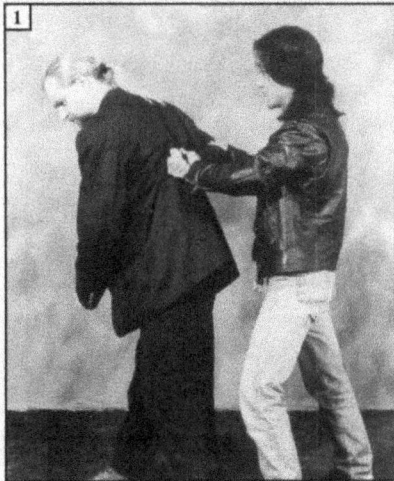

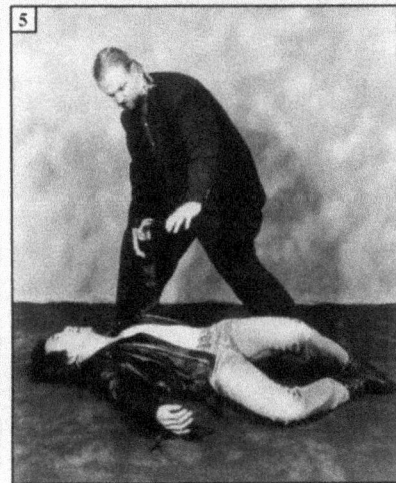

You are held in a back arm lock (1). You do not struggle, but pivot in the direction of your free arm; not against the hold (2). You strike your opponent to his head with your elbow. Continuing through with your striking arm(3), you reach it around your opponent's neck, as you extend your leg in front of his (4). You throw him to the ground (5).

WEAPONS

Violent street crime has come, more and more, to be linked directly with the use of weapons. Knives and guns have become readily available. So much so, that the majority of street criminals possess them. Therefore, we must develop an understanding of how to effectively countermand their seemingly deadly force.

First of all, it is far better to leave a situation where your assailant is wielding a weapon than to choose to encounter him. If this is not possible, then, the second course of action is to defend yourself rapidly with no holds barred; as he obviously has no concern for your safety

As each situation holds its own set of rules and limitation, there is no universal method to defend against the assault of a weapon. There is, however a few basic courses of action that will assure victory in many situations. The leading rule is to keep all defensive techniques as simple as possible.

When accosted by an opponent who possesses a knife; never move to him. If he remains at a safe distance, let that distance remain, as that is a clear safety zone. For by rushing in at him, he has the advantage of holding the knife and may easily cut you as you move forward.

"Violent street crime has come, more and more, to be linked directly with the use of weapons."

If the knife assailant is in close proximity to you, then you must take immediate action as your safety is no doubt in question.

It is very common among knife fighters that they move their weapon around in an attempt to intimidate their victims. You can use this movement to your advantage by studying the movements of the hand and arm holding the weapon. As the knife is moving away from you, this is the time to strike. First, deflect the arm of the opponent which holds the knife, by pushing it inward towards his body. Leave your blocking hand or arm in place checking the possible movement of your assailant's knife.

By doing this you have limited the knife's effectiveness in immediately cutting you. Then, you must immediately powerfully strike your opponent; generally to his head, in one of the key impact points; being his eyes, temples, throat, or a palm strike under his nose. To strike to any other less debilitating region, is

57

Your opponent has you in a head lock (1). You strike to his groin with a reverse knife hand (2). You then grab him by the back of his hair thus locking his neck (3), as you lift him at knee level (4), throwing him back to the ground (5).

fruitless, as he will then have the ability to quickly come back at you.

Once you have performed this initial self defense technique against the knife, you should never attempt to directly take the blade away from your assailant. By reaching in and attempting to do so, you give him the ability to cut your hand as you reach Therefore, you must continue on with appropriate, repetitive strikes to his body until he is completely disabled.

Guns, even more deadly than knifes, are prevalent more and more on our streets. As they are much more deadly defense against them must be even more precise than that of the knife.

The gun can not be effectively defended against if your opponent is any distance from you Never rush in at an opponent with a gun If they are close, a hand gun can be deflected in a similar fashion as the previously mentioned knife defense technique.

"You should never attempt to directly take the blade away from your assailant."

All care must be taken, as a bullet, once a trigger is pulled, can mean instant death to yourself or others standing around you

If an assailant has accosted you from behind it is common that they will announce they have a pistol by placing its barrel against your back. At the moment you feels its presence, is the time to take action. By immediately spinning around deflecting the weapon outwards to a range where it can not shoot you, you must immediately strike the opponent with a palm hand strike under his nose or a similar technique. Thus, you will have successfully defended yourself

An opponent who accosts you on the street has no moral values, with this in mind set, we must put all visions of John Wayne and a very fair fight out of the way When it comes to your safety you must do what ever it takes to protect yourself On the street it is a "no holds barred" situation. Your opponent isn't going to abide by any rules, neither should you.

Confrontations are to no ones advantage. Self defense, however is an absolute necessity as a means to assure yourself and your loved ones that you may continue safely forward with your lives.

Hapkido

'In-Fighting'

No matter at what distance your assailant begins his confrontation with you, it is not until you are virtually nose-to-nose with him that the actual physical part of the brawl will take place. Knowing this, we must first of all understand that street altercations are not at all like the ethical and fair sparring matches in the martial art studio or sanctioned fights in the ring.

No matter at what distance your assailant begins his confrontation with you, it is not until you are virtually nose-to-nose with him that the actual physical part of the brawl will take place. Knowing this, we must first of all understand that street altercations are not at all like the ethical and fair sparring matches in the martial art studio or sanctioned fights in the ring. It is for this reason so many highly trained martial artists are rapidly over powered in a fight by a savvy street fighter once the distance is closed between the two of them and the 'in-fighting' begins.

In a street fight, your opponent is going to rush in at you and the entire fight is going to be won or lost in that very close range. Therefore, you must learn to effectively and rapidly deal with your opponent's aggression the moment he closes the distance between the two of you.

On the street, you do not have the luxury, as you do in the Dojo or fighting ring, to block your opponent's initial attack, then momentarily retreat to launch a powerful kicking or similar offensive assault at him. On the street it is close contact, non stop fighting, and you need to be prepared for it.

Traditionally, once an attacking opponent charges in at you, continually punching him may have the eventual desired effect of achieving victory over him. One or even two rapidly delivered punches, however, is rarely enough to completely disable your opponent. Without immediately disabling him, he has the ability to launch a powerful secondary attack at you. Therefore, we as martial artists, must investigate more effective ways to deal with an opponent's close contact aggressions.

Your opponent has rushed in at you. He grabs you by your shoulder He powerfully punches you in the ribs. Instead of attempting to block his punching attacks, you should instead rapidly move into your own offensive action. Thereby, you have the ability to not only immediately take control of the altercations but not waste energy on a blocking technique which may or may not be effective against his next hit. This is especially the case if his initial punching attack is launched at your body and will have a minimal damaging effect.

Instead of blocking, let's examine a more effective way of dealing with an opponent who has closed the distance on you, taken a hold of your shoulder and is possibly punching to your ribs. To immediately take control of this fight, you can powerfully palm strike your opponent to the side of his nose, by reaching your arm over your opponent's grabbing arm. This strike, not only has the very probable ability of breaking your opponent's nose but it will, at the least, momentarily halt his attack.

In the Korean martial art of Hapkido we learn that, any defensive technique should always be preceded by a strike to a vital region on your opponent. These focused preliminary strikes, possess the ability to not only injure your opponent but will leave him stunned and thus halt his attack for at least a moment. This momentary lapse in attack, will give you the time you need to effectively strike again or to lock or throw him so he does not have the ability to continue his attack on you.

59

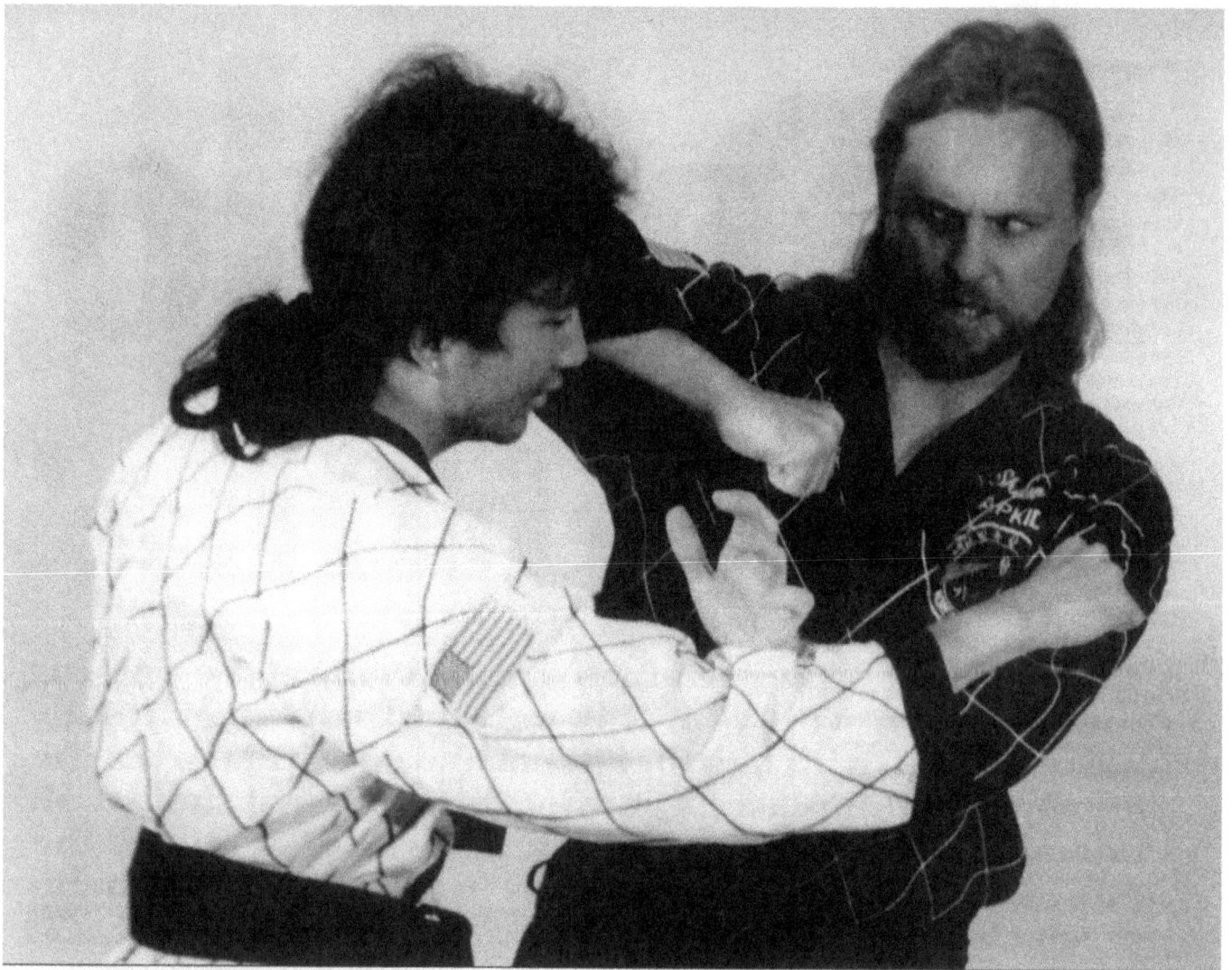

The Hapkido vital strike points, which ideally pertain to close contact in-fighting are the nose, the temples, the eyes, under the jaw, the knees, and the groin. The reason Hapkido believes you should isolate any and all of your strikes is that this makes each one of them an effective weapon, instead of just the random body and facial hits which are dished out in the common street fight.

Once you have made this initial cross nose palm strike, your opponent is stunned. You can then, immediately, with little opposition, reach in and grab your opponent's head; with one hand under his jaw in the front and your other hand behind his head. Then, by slightly arching his neck, locking it into place, you can easily direct him to the ground, or if you wish to maintain additional control over him, take him in a powerful head lock.

As we see in-fighting does not have to be a random, "may the better man win," type of confrontation. By using the close proximity of your opponent to your own advantage, you can easily emerge victorious from the fight.

Though you now understand blocking an opponent's attempts to punch at you is not necessary to your overall victory in a close contact confrontation, it does feel much better if you never get hit at all. Therefore, if you need to make punch blocking your initial course of action to stop attacks, especially to your head, you should not simply block, but utilize that block to your overall advantage at winning the confrontation. To achieve this you must combine any block immediately with additional defensive maneuvers.

Your adversary, in a rage, grabs a hold of you. He is attempting to strike at you with a roundhouse punch, (the most common punch on the street). As the roundhouse punch is very pronounced, slow, and easily seen, you can rapidly block its oncoming path with an in-to-out knife hand block. By leaving your blocking hand in place, at your opponent's elbow level, you keep him from launching a secondary attack with that arm.

Immediately, upon blocking his punch, you can strike your opponent to his temples

with an elbow strike, delivered by your non blocking arm. This elbow strike will have an obviously debilitating effect on your opponent. Now, that you have gotten your opponent's attention by elbow striking him to his temples, you must immediately follow through with additional offensive techniques to assure your victory.

Once you have made the elbow strike, you can allow your arm to continue through and then immediately come back and back fist or knife hand strike him to his face. Your opponent, after receiving these two powerful vital point strikes, will obviously be dazed. You can now effortlessly throw him to the ground by grabbing, at both of his shoulders and powerfully directing him in that direction; where, if necessary, you can launch additional attacks.

Hapkido teaches, in any fighting situation, you should stay in continual motion; immediately moving from one technique on to the next, until your opponent is completely disabled. As we have just seen, this is the case with first blocking his punch, then immediately

60

moving forward with powerful strikes, leading to a throw.

Many traditional martial art systems teach the "blow by blow" theory; block or strike and then wait to see what effect you have had. This type of fighting philosophy is far to slow for a street encounter An enraged attacker will continue forward unstopping, with random, often times wild, fighting techniques at you. For this reason, you should not allow your opponent the possibility of hurting you and gaining the advantage in the fight by waiting to see what effect each technique you have delivered is having.

Often times, you may have the ability to end a fight before it even starts. If an opponent is actually rushing at you, rapidly closing the distance, you can use his motion to your own advantage. In Hapkido, it is taught, if you have the option, it is always to your advantage to deflect an attack as opposed to encountering it directly.

Your opponent rushes at you; simply by side stepping his oncoming grab and deflecting his arms to one side of you, so that he can not easily take hold of your clothing, you can use his own momentum and direct him downwards where you can introduce him to a powerful knee strike. Though you could, just as easily, deflect his momentum, in the same fashion, and send him crashing forward with his own motion. It is far better, however, to take advantage of your first strike ability and to not allow your opponent to have the second chance at hitting you, he may gain, by not immediately taking control and striking him.

An enraged attacker may not choose to fight you with punches. He may instead, attempt to over power you by quickly closing in and attempting to choke you. This is

1) Your opponent has grabbed you and is punching you in the ribs. 2) You palm strike him across his nose. 3) You then, immediately, lock his neck as you 4) grab him in a choke hold.

1) Your opponent rushes at you. 2) You deflect his arms to one side as you use his own momentum and 3) direct him into your knee strike.

61

often times the case, if he has the ability to shove you up against a wall as he is choking. Instead of awkwardly attempting to pull yourself free, you can use his own positioning to your advantage.

As he is choking you, his head is just a few inches from yours. By rapidly upper cut punching his jaw, you will not only loosen any grasp he has on you, but you will stun him, if not knock him out altogether

Now that his choke hold is loosened and he is dazed, he is quite easily dealt with. You can easily smash his head against the wall he has you pinned against or send him to the ground, by simply reaching your arm over his arms, while extending your leg as leverage, and direct him towards the floor

As we have just come to understand, the uppercut punch is one of the most effective punches you can use while in-fighting. Therefore, you have to be very careful you do not allow your opponent the ability to use this technique on you. How then can you prevent your opponent from upper cut punching you in a close contact bout?

Your opponent has grabbed hold of you. He is about to unleash an upper cut punch at your jaw. You halt the progress of this punch by delivering a powerful cross arm knife hand to his elbow joint. This not only halts the progress of the punch but keeps his arm from unleashing a secondary attack at you, as well.

By leaving your knife hand in place, you can utilize this elbow joint lock to your advantage. You rapidly grab your opponent's shoulder, in a cross arm fashion. You now possess a two handed grasp on him. While pivoting his body around, so that you can place a leg behind his to use as a throwing tool, you pull him in tightly to your body, to keep him from launching any possible kicking or kneeling techniques. Now that your leg is positioned behind his, you can effectively direct him to the ground by pushing him over it. Once on the ground, you will be on top of him and able to unleash whichever offensive action you find necessary.

As we have seen, by putting traditional fighting methods aside, you can take the random acts of violence which occur in the average close contact street fight and use your opponent's aggressive actions to your own advantage. By first hitting to vital strike points and then following through with continuous motion until your opponent is completely disabled, you will emerge victorious from any 'in-fighting' situation you may find yourself.

1) Your opponent has grabbed you and is attempting to roundhouse punch you. 2) You block his punch with a knife hand block. 3) Immediately, you elbow strike him to his face. 4) You continue through and knife hand strike him to his nose. 5) You can then, effortlessly 6) send him to the ground.

KNEE FIGHTING

Close contact fighting has always proven to be one of the most complicated situations a martial artist can find himself in.

by Scott Shaw

Close contact fighting has always proved to be one of the most complicated situations a martial artist can find himself in. The reason it is difficult to rapidly and successfully defend yourself, once your opponent has moved closely in on you and possibly taken a hold of your clothing, is because in close proximity your available counter strike techniques become very limited. First of all, there is not enough distance between your body and that of your opponent's to effectively kick him. And, with the exception of the upper-cut punch, your punching defense is limited to wildly thrown roundhouse punches which at best will make contact with the side of your opponent's head. There is, however, an effective method to close

contact "in-fighting" which many martial artists do not fully investigate or develop. That method is the use of the knee as a powerful striking weapon.

The knee strike is an excellent close proximity fighting tool. This is because there is not much space needed to make its attack effective.

A knee strike takes no advanced training to perform. There is, however certain limitations to the use of the knee. Therefore, we must fully explore the science of knee fighting to first gain knowledge of what not to do, before we can understand what the knee can effectively accomplish.

The knee is one of the most sensitive joints on the human body. It is quite easily damaged. When you strike with the knee, it

is very important you do so in the proper manner. For if you perform a knee strike improperly, you stand the chance of injuring your knee instead of defending yourself successfully.

Your knee should always be bent when you attack with it. By bending your knee, you not only isolate its impact point but keep it from bending unnaturally against itself; tearing your ligaments, cartilage, or in more severe cases, breaking your knee altogether

A knee strike should never be delivered in a side to side format. This is to say, never attempt to impact with the side of your knee. The side area of your knee joint is very sensitive and your lower leg can easily be sent in the opposite direction of your upper

leg if you incorrectly attempt to strike with it in this fashion.

The part of your knee which should be used as a striking weapon is the upper part. Reach down to your thigh and follow your upper leg muscle to the point where it meets the knee bone; this is the ideal strike point for knee attacks.

A proper knee strike is accomplished by rapidly lifting your knee up and into its target. The power of the knee strike is initiated at the hip, and is driven forward with the muscles of the upper leg.

The first strike point most people think of when utilizing a knee attack is the opponent's groin. This is, in fact, a good location to aim for especially if your opponent has grabbed you in a straight forward choke hold or similar frontal attack. In this type of attack, your opponent's groin region is easily accessible and a powerful knee strike can make instantaneous contact and lead you to victory in the confrontation.

Though the knee can virtually strike any location on your opponent's body, given the right set of circumstances, there are several location which are ideal knee strike targets; they are: the groin, the ribs, the kidneys, under the opponent's jaw, and to a lesser degree, the inside of the opponent's upper leg. The time to strike at these various targets is only dominated by the type of encounter you find yourself in.

One of the most important thing to remember when using the knee as a weapon is, you should never use your knee to strike at a location on your opponent's body where you have to travel to. This is to say that the knee strike is not an ideal long distance reaching weapon; as is the case with the various punching techniques and many of the traditional martial art kicks. This is due to the fact that the very elements that make the knee an ideal close contact weapon, makes it inefficient in distance applications.

The knee can not reach out as does the arm or leg. As well, if you leave the knee in a "cocked to strike" position and attempt to launch yourself, at a distance, in towards your opponent with the momentum you can gain from jumping off of your non-knee kicking leg, you not only leave yourself in an off balance position, but you will be leaving your body open and exposed to powerful attacks from your opponent, as well. Therefore, the use of the knee as a striking weapon should be limited to close quarter "in-fighting."

A well placed knee strike is dominated by two factors; one, is it an easily reachable target and the second, will the strike you

1) Your opponent punches at you. 2) You deflect his attack with an into-out block. 3) You take a hold of his punching arm and 4) pull him down to meet your knee attack to his solar plexus.

make with your knee have the debilitating effect on our opponent you desire? If the answer to both of these questions is yes, then that is the time to perform a powerful knee strike.

Now that we understand the basics of the science of knee fighting, we can investigate the best knee fighting tactics in order that we may efficiently and effectively knee strike our opponent in each applicable situation.

As previously mentioned, when grabbed in a forward hold, a knee to your opponent's groin is a very effective defensive measure. But, what can you do in the few seconds before your opponent has actually taken a hold of you; especially if his intentions are obviously violent and he is moving quickly in your direction?

First of all, it is never a good idea to allow an opponent to grab a hold of you, if you have the option. Therefore, when an opponent is rapidly moving towards you, this affords you an

ideal opportunity to use his momentum to your own advantage. This is accomplished in one of two ways. The first method of achieving momentum advantage over your adversary, as he closes in on you, is by deflecting his arms outward, with an in-to-out knife hand block, once he is close enough. After this deflection has been performed, you can maintain substantial control over his movements by grabbing a hold of his elbow region, once his arm has been blocked. By first deflecting his arms outward, while allowing his momentum to continue forward, you have opened his body up for you to easily attack him with a powerful knee strike.

Though this deflection leading to a knee strike happens in a second, with the momentum the two of you have gained by moving towards one another you can powerfully knee strike him either in his groin, solar plexus, or easily launch yourself upward and deliver a very debilitating knee strike under his jaw.

65

The second avenue we can take for an oncoming opponent, who is either attempting to grab or strike at us is to deflect his extending arm inwards, with an out-to-in forearm block. Once his arm has been deflected, you should maintain a controlling hand on his elbow, so he can not perform a secondary strike at you with say a back fist. By performing this type of block, you allow your opponent to continue through with his own forward motion. Thus, leaving his forward ribs or back exposed to an easy counter attack with your knee.

In this case, if it is most effective for you to strike at his ribs, you simply allow his motion to continue as you guide him down by taking control of his extended arm, as your knee powerfully meets his ribs. If you choose to knee strike his kidneys you can simply deflect his arm and allow his developed momentum to continue him moving forward, slightly past you; thus, exposing

his back to your powerful knee attack.

As the key to all successful defense is to strike your opponent before he has the opportunity to strike you, knee fighting is no different. Therefore, now that we understand how we can easily open our opponent's body up for knee strikes, let's evaluate how we can effectively maintain control over him, while we are accomplishing a debilitating knee attack.

Whenever you are going to use your knee as your initial form of self defense, in close contact "in-fighting," you must do two things. First of all, as we now understand, the knee is not a good weapon at a distance. For this reason we must keep our opponent from retreating or moving back out of the way of the effective knee strike range. The most efficient way to accomplish this, is to take a hold of him in order to keep him from moving out of the range of your impending knee strike. Secondarily,

once you have set yourself up to knee strike your opponent, you must keep him from powerfully counter striking you in the process of your knee attack. To do this, there are three areas of his body you must become very aware of; they are: his arms, legs, and head.

If you control an opponent's elbows, you can effectively control his entire body. Thus, as we have learned in the previous examples of deflecting any grabbing or striking attack on the part of our opponent, we should either leave our block in place at his elbow level or grab his arm so we can keep him from launching any secondary hand strike.

As no rule holds undisputed for all fighting situations, maintaining an elbow block or grasp while continuing through with your knee assault may not always be possible. If elbow control is not feasible, the secondary locations which you should concentrate your attentions on to give you added control over your opponent is his shoulder or wrist region.

By grasping at or leaving your arm in ready position at your opponent's shoulder level, you can quickly foil any oncoming fist attack while your knee strike is in progress. The same is true in the case of a grasp at or near your opponent's wrist.

Not only by taking control of your opponent's arm, once his initial attack has been deflected, do you control his ability to strike at you again, but by controlling his arms you also can effectively guide him to your desired knee strike location. This opponent guidance is accomplished either by using his own forward momentum and passively directing him to your desired knee strike or by forcefully pulling him downwards by his arms, powerfully onto your knee, once you have deflected his initial attack.

Commonly, in professional kickboxing, knee attacks are launched to the inside of an opponent's leg. Though the legs of an opponent should always be monitored in a street altercation, there are two very serious problems with using your opponent's legs as knee strike focal points. First of all, this type of attack does little debilitating damage to your opponent, so there is virtually no point in using it as an attack zone in a street confrontation. Secondarily, by moving in that close to your opponent, if you have not taken effective control of his arms, he has the ability to powerfully strike you with his fists or elbows. Therefore, this is not an ideal primary strike point for knee fighting.

1) Your opponent attempts to punch at you. 2) You block in the same fashion, taking control of his head. 3) You propel yourself upwards, multiplying the impact to your opponent's head, 4) as you lift your body from the ground.

1) Your opponent attempts to punch you. 2) You block his assault with an in-to-out knife hand block at his elbow level. 3) Immediately, your blocking hand slides behind his head, 4) pulling it down. 5) You knee kick him to his face.

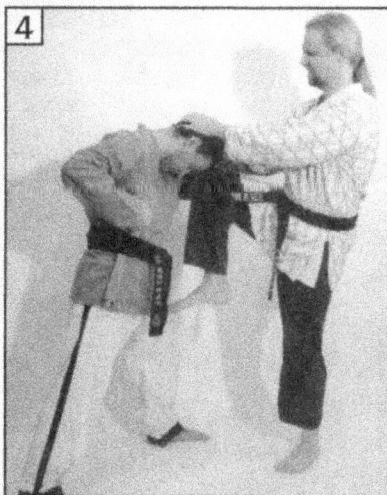

Finally, in controlling your opponent in order to effectively knee strike him, there is no better source of control than his neck and head region. This region is easily accessible, especially in the case of close contact "in fighting" as your two bodies are already in close proximity.

To effectively take control of your opponent's motions is as easy as rapidly reaching in and grabbing him in a frontal grip by his throat. This type of grab will not only momentarily distract him as to your strategic intentions, but will allow you to maintain control over his movements long enough to powerfully knee strike him in the groin.

Controlling your opponent's head is equally easily accomplished. You should go for head control immediately after you have deflected your opponent's arm out of its forward aggressive motion. At this second, your opponent's initial attack has been nullified and he is most prone for a rapid and unexpected counter defense. Once deflected, you can strongly grab a hold of your opponent's head, with one or both of your hands, and shove it downward, in position, for a jumping knee strike to his face.

Traditionally, martial art schools have advised that once your opponent has moved in tight on your body, you should attempt to shove him back in order to effectively kick him or deliver a powerful punching technique. Attempting to utilize this type of defense promises limited results, however This is especially the case if your opponent has already taken a powerful hold of your clothing or does so in the process of being shoved back. As we have learned with the use of the properly placed knee, there is not a need to expend unnecessary energy, attempting to shove or grapple with your opponent. Simply deliver a well placed knee attack and your opponent will be instantly injured. At this point, if necessary, you can effortlessly continue with further counter attacks.

1) Your opponent grabs you in a forward choke hold. 2) You take a hold of his shoulders to maintain control over him, as you knee strike him to the groin.

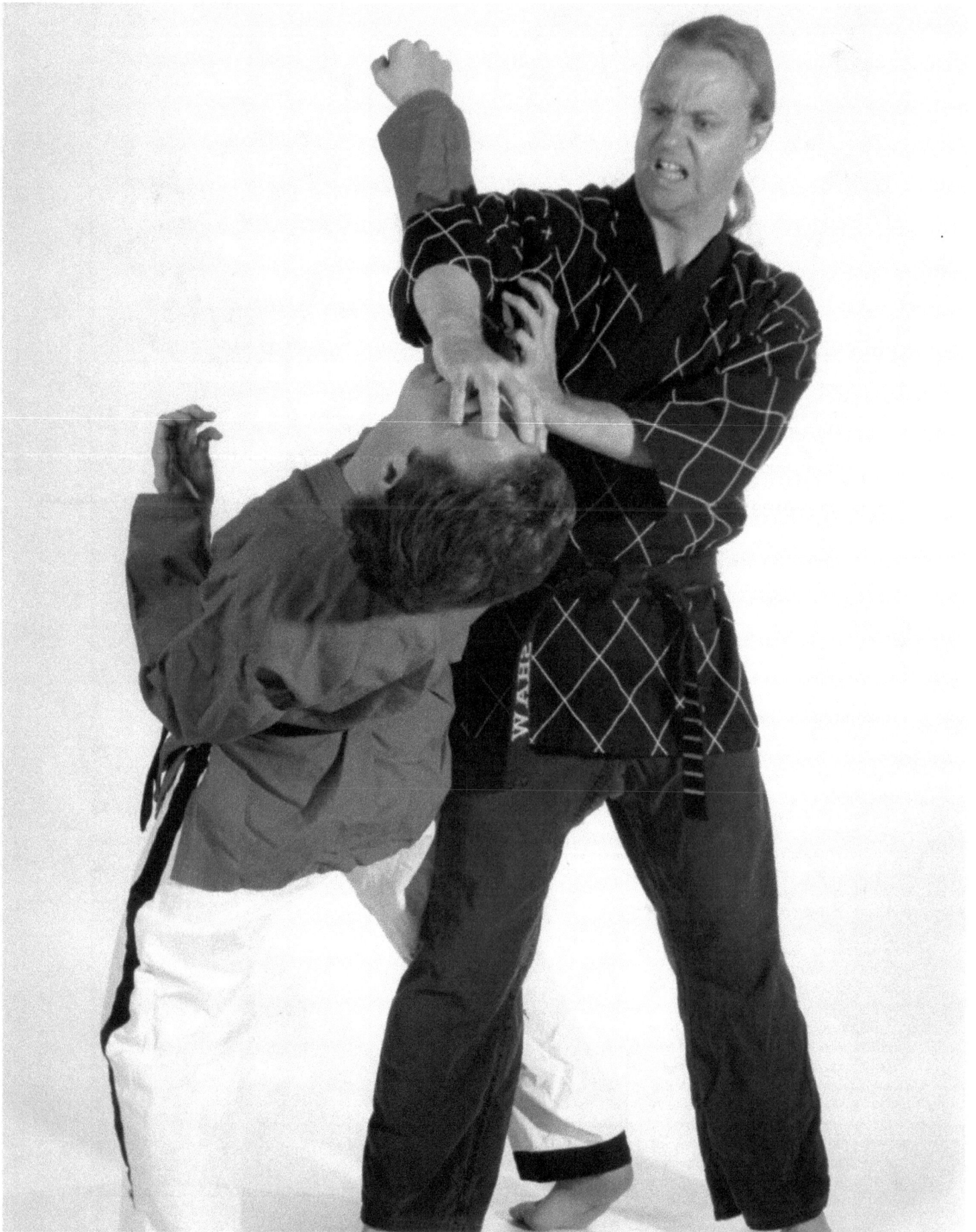

Hapkido, Strategy Against the Street Punch

One of Korea's Most Complete Martial Arts vs. the Sucker Puncher

By Scott Shaw

The common punch is undoubtedly one of the most universally used offensive weapons any of us will run up against in a street confrontation. Though most martial art schools teach us various formal blocks to encounter an opponent's launched punch; this type of expected training is far too sterile for the wild and random punches an opponent will throw at you on the street. For this reason, to come to understand what is truly effective, in terms of self defense in a street confrontation when an assailant attacks us with a punching offense, we must

study the elements that make up a punch and thereby come to understand how we can best defend against this most common type of attack.

To begin our study of the punch we must initially view the effective ranges and how to most easily deal with the two basic types of street punches that exist; which are: the straight punch and the more wildly delivered, yet more common, roundhouse punch. To achieve this understanding it is most effective for you to work with a training partner and first have him launch his punching attacks at

you slowly and then speed them up as you become more familiar with their individual ranges, limitations, and how they are most effectively dealt with.

First of all have your training partner perform a straight punch, directed at your face. What is your initial course of action? What is generally done and is no doubt the leading mistake most novices and long trained martial artists alike attempt to do, when a standard straight punch is launched at them, is to forcefully block it. Though this is the generally prescribed method in most martial art

69

form of self defense for the competent martial artist.

To illustrate the folly of attempting to forcefully block your opponent's on coming straight punch, allow him to strike quickly and forcefully at your head, with a straight punch technique (preferably while he wears boxing gloves and you wear head protection). Now, attempt to block this punch with whatever traditional technique you may have been trained in. What happens nine out of ten times when you attempt to block his strike in the traditional way is that you will be hit.

"The straight punch by its very nature is linear in design and application."

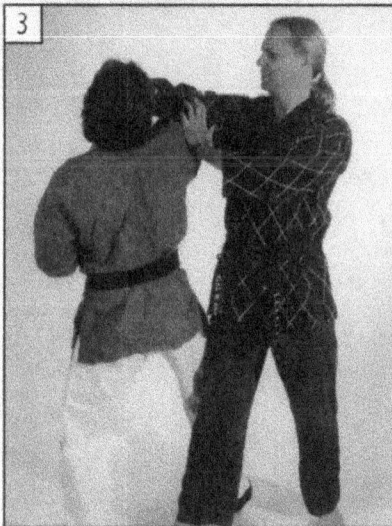

Your opponent attempts a straight punch at you (1). You side step its impact point and deflect it (2). Then, while your arm checks your opponent's arm, so he can not use it to strike at you again, you rapidly reach your blocking arm over his punching arm and grab his face (3). You then powerfully shove him to the ground over your lead leg (4).

systems; to do this, you must meet power with power bone to bone.

Though you may in fact block the punch, what also may occur as has been illustrated time and time again, is that you will injure yourself in the process, due to the forceful contact of the strike impacting to whatever part of your body it encounters.

The Korean martial art of Hapkido teaches that it is not a good idea to block any oncoming offensive technique with a solid blocking technique, as do many of the more linear martial art forms. The reason it is believed to not be advisable, is that if you meet aggressive force with a traditional block you may very well damage the part of your body which you have blocked the attack with, due to the

force of the opponent's striking impact to that region of your body.

Furthermore, by forcefully blocking an attack, especially that of a punching technique, often times you lock yourself so deeply into that defensive maneuver that it is difficult to move forward with additional counter defensive or offensive measures. If you cannot quickly move forward with additional techniques, your opponent may well have the ability to strike you again, this time more successfully and perhaps win the confrontation. To this end, it is imperative that you make any defensive technique you perform free enough that you may quickly move on to additional techniques, if necessary Thus, it is not recommended that the traditional punch block be the initial

The straight punch by its very nature is linear in design and application. Its force is derived from the expelling of power from the central axis of the body. The well delivered straight punch is not only one of the most powerful elements in the trained martial artists hand arsenal, it is also one of the hardest punches to effectively block, as well; no matter how precisely developed your blocking technique may be. This is due to the fact that this punch drives forward on a linear path from a directed central point onto a specific impact point and it does not need much developed motion to deliver a powerful impact. There is however effective defensive methods to effectively deal with the straight punch, other than by simply blocking it.

Let's try viewing the oncoming straight punch in a new manner: not simply as something to attempt to forcefully block or get struck by but simply as an oncoming object that we would avoid, similar to that of a stinging bee.

This time, have your opponent attempt a straight punch at you. Now, instead of directly encountering it with a traditional blocking technique, simply rapidly side step the punch while it is moving forward towards you.

What occurs? First of all the punch will miss you. Secondarily the momentum developed by the force of your opponent's

continuing through with the power of his own motion, thus, again, leaving him prone for a counter attack.

The roundhouse punch develops its power through circular movement. Its force is multiplied by the distance between its initial swing and impact point. Therefore, by stepping back out of its range, this allows the punch to develop full power; which, once it has missed its target traps it user into clumsily continuing through with his own motion.

What we have learned from the above illustrations, is there is often times no need to forcefully block a punching assault from your opponent at all. It is not only simpler but far safer to quickly move out of the way of any oncoming punching technique, allowing it to miss its impact point on your body altogether. Further-

more, by not actually forcefully blocking the punching technique of your opponent, we have seen how the momentum he developed by launching the assault against you, forces him to continue through with his own motion, leaving him open for a rapid counter attack.

Certainly, we all understand with the wildly thrown punches that generally occur in a street confrontation we may indeed need to block them; even forcefully at times, though we now understand it may not be to our best advantage.

In the event a block is necessary against an offensive punching technique, your first attempt should be a punch block that deflects the opponent's energy, rather than directly encountering it. By deflecting your opponent's energy, instead of encountering it "head on," you may again utilize his

"The roundhouse punch develops its power through circular movement."

Your opponent attempts a straight punch at you (1). You side step it and deflect it (2). While holding his arm in check you reach your other arm under his punching arm and impact him to his neck with a reverse knife hand (3). By pivoting, you throw him to the ground (4).

punch makes him continue through with his own motion, leaving him in a vulnerable position for a counter attack. As you have stepped out of the way of the oncoming punch, no injury occurred to you or any part of your body and you used virtually no energy in your defense against it.

Now that we understand the basic elements of the straight punch, let's shift our attention to the most common punch used in the street, that of the roundhouse punch. Have your training partner perform a roundhouse punch; again, directed at your head. As he performs the punch, quickly step back and out of the range of the oncoming strike. Again, the punch misses you and the momentum your opponent has developed has him

Your opponent attempts a roundhouse punch at you (1). You step back out of its reach and deflect it at his elbow level (2). You then, rapidly, kick to his head with an inside front kick (3).

own expended energy against himself and to your own advantage.

Deflection is accomplished in different ways with different punches. For example, in the case of a straight punch, it is most successfully implemented by initially following the procedure described earlier and simply side stepping the punches impending force, as you move slightly forward in the direction of your opponent. While doing this, you should deflect the punch with either an in-to-out forearm block or an in-to-out knife hand deflection; using the arm that is closest to your opponent, as this will be the fastest element of your body to reach his punching arm and it requires the least amount of energy on your part. Once your opponent's straight punch is deflected he will then continue through with his own momentum, as previously described.

The reason that you should move slightly forward as you deflect a straight punch in this fashion, is three fold; one, it aids in your opponent's continued momentum of his own energy; two, it leaves you in the least vulnerable position for him to launch a secondary attack, and three, it places you is a superior positioning for counter attacking.

It is imperative when deflecting an opponent's attack that he is not only left in a less than optimum position for launching a secondary attack on you but that you are left in the superior posting to make a successful counter attack on him. Therefore, what gives you the advantage in a street confrontation when you are encountering a punching opponent and deflecting his attacks, is that you have come to understand, through partner practice, what techniques

> # "Deflection is accomplished in different ways with different punches."

effectively deflect each punch, while utilizing the least amount of energy on your part, thus leaving you in control of the confrontation.

Certainly no one believes you will always be able to simply step out of the way of a punch or deflect a barrage of oncoming punches from a wildly driven opponent. However to insure your own safety, your defensive strategy against the various degrees of a punching attack should take place as follows: First, step out of the way of the oncoming punch. If this is not applicable due to environment or physical constraints then deflect oncoming punches. If your opponent continues on wildly with his attack and your initial counter attacks have been unsuccessful then, when necessary, to save yourself from being hit by impending strikes, block the punch by any means possible.

If simply moving out of the way of a punch is not achievable, due to environmental or physical constraints, and a force-

ful punch block is necessary, the key element to remember is to always block your opponent at his elbow region. For if you control your opponent's elbow, you control his entire body.

Try this example with your training partner: allow him to roundhouse punch at you. Again, step slightly back out of the range of the assault, as previously discussed. Now, once the punch has missed you, rapidly move in on him and lightly hold his striking arm at his elbow level. If he attempts to move it, put more pressure on it. As you will see, this simple technique allows you a large amount of control over your opponent's body. It additionally allows you to effectively and powerfully counter strike him, as you hold him in place for a moment.

The circular nature of a roundhouse punch, by its very design, allows itself to been seen, as it is set up, long before it is actually executed. The power of this punch comes from the momentum it gains from its swing. As this is the nature of the roundhouse punch, there is of course times when, through training, you will see it coming and want to block it, as near to its inception point as possible, in order to open your opponent up for a powerful counter attack.

To gain the proper understanding of the timing involved in this, allow your opponent to strike at you again with a roundhouse punch. This time, do not move back out of the way of the oncoming strike but quickly step into it, blocking the punch in a into-out fashion either with a knife hand or forearm block to the inside of your opponent's elbow region. Again, you will witness how you have gained control of his arm.

To gain optimum results in directly block-

ing the roundhouse punch, it must be encountered as close to its point of inception as possible; for then your opponent will not have had the opportunity to develop much force in his swing. Therefore, the block will be much easier to perform.

In the case of blocking a roundhouse punch inside, as described, your opponent may attempt to strike at you with his other arm, as you are vulnerable to that type of secondary attack once you have blocked the punch in this fashion. Therefore, you must be prepared and be able to move into further defense against another punch, with a similar blocking technique, if necessary.

The final way of quickly, easily, and effectively dealing with a punching opponent is to rapidly rush in on top of his attack. Thus, leaving him no room to punch. By doing this, you not only crowd his ability to

develop any power in his punching offense but it will no doubt throw him off balance. As this type of crowding defense is rarely used, few have the ability to quickly recover from its onslaught. The draw back to this type of punch defense is that if you do not immediately launch a counter attack, once you are that closely inside, your opponent may grab a hold of you and you could end up in a grappling match on the ground, which is to no one's advantage. Therefore, you must rapidly come in ready to execute a knee attack or perhaps a palm hand strike to your opponent's face.

In Hapkido, no defensive technique is ever performed without the appropriate counter assault being immediately launched at your opponent. This is the large difference between this art and its distant relative Aikido. As a street confrontation is generally

never won simply by avoiding or blocking your opponent's attack; for this reason you must always be prepared to rapidly and powerfully counter attack your opponent.

It is important to understand how easy and effective these counter attacks can be in punching defense situations. To this end, again square off with your practice opponent and allow him to punch at you. In regards to the straight punch, once you have deflected or side stepped the punch, you are in an optimum position to easily side kick your opponent to the side of his knee. In the case of the roundhouse punch, once you have stepped from its reach, you can either front kick your opponent to his groin or rapidly move in on him, checking his elbow, and straight punch him to his face.

Of course, this type of very direct counter attack may not suit the defensive situation

"The final way of quickly, easily, and effectively dealing with a punching opponent is to rapidly rush in on top of his attack."

Your opponent attempts to roundhouse punch you (1). You step inside of it and block to the inside of his elbow (2). You then grab a hold of his punching arm (3) as you instantly strike him to his throat with a knife hand (4). As you continue through with it power of the strike, you throw him to the ground aided by your own leg which has stepped inside his (5).

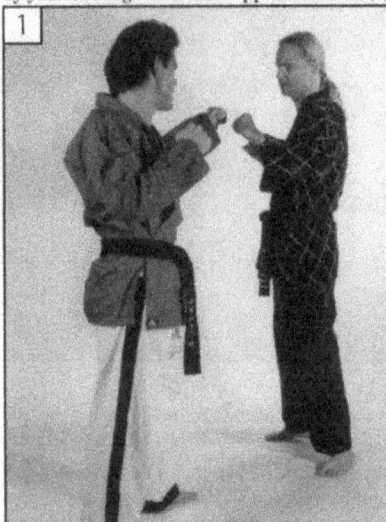

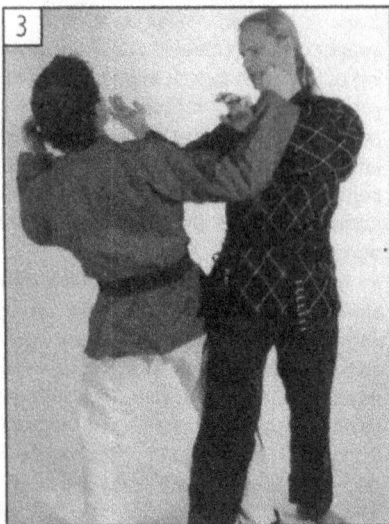

Your opponent attempts to roundhouse punch you (1). You block to the inside of his elbow (2). He immediately attempts to punch you with his other fist (3). You block that punch in the same fashion (4). By grabbing a hold of his clothing, he can not easily break free (5). You knee him to his groin (6). Then, with the aid of your grab, you deliver a powerful head butt to the bridge of his nose (7).

you find yourself in. Therefore, you may wish to effectively throw your opponent to the ground. This can be equally easily accomplished. In the situation of the straight punch, once you deflect it, in the manner discussed earlier by quickly reaching your blocking arm under or over his punching arm, you can impact your opponent at throat level with a reverse knife hand. Then, simply by continuing pressure at his neck level and pivoting him over your forward leg, he is thrown to the ground.

In the case of the roundhouse punch, once his initial punch has been nullified by an in-to-out knife hand block at his elbow level, you can have your blocking arm instantly grab his arm, thus holding it in place, while you rapidly knife hand strike him in the throat with your other hand. Then, by stepping around his leg and pivoting, you easily throw him to the ground.

If your initial counter attack is ineffective or if your adversary continues on with a barrage of punches, you must rapidly deal with the situation so his continued strikes at you will not have the cumulative effect of his winning the confrontation. Therefore, if a wild punching attack ensues, step rapidly back away from the impact of the continuing punches, allowing at least one punch to pass in front of you. From here, rapidly move in and powerfully strike him with your most powerful hand or leg technique. For letting a confrontation continue longer than is necessary is only to the advantage of the aggressor

As we have learned, once we understand the elements which make up the various street punches, they are easily and effectively dealt with; while never needing to resort to the less than efficient traditional power blocks. From this knowledge we have not only become more competent fighters but better martial artists, as well.

Hapkido
Defense with a Vengeance

A bully grabs you by the collar and pulls you toward him. You have one of two options: you can allow his aggression to continue and ask for him to release you. This, however, may end in your own ultimate demise. Or, second, you can allow his own energy to pull you forward while you step around his leg, causing him to become unbalanced. Now, strike him in his throat. Thus, you have crippled his attack and he falls, defeated, to the ground. The confrontation has ended immediately, to your advantage.

By Scott Shaw, Ph.D.
Photos by Joel Ciniero

apkido, one of the central Korean martial arts has, as one of its key defense elements, "Total penetration and control of an adversary's offense and defense." This is accomplished not only by using an opponent's own energy against himself, but by counterstriking, with full power, to end a conflict before it has the chance to continue further.

Hapkido is thought by many to be derived from the passive Japanese martial art of Aikido. This is not the case. Aikido is predominantly a defensive art. Hapkido, on the other hand, not only redirects an opponent's energy, as does Aikido, but then counter-strikes with powerful force as well.

Hapkido's First Priority

Modern Hapkido was developed by Yong-shul Choi in the early 20th century In 1910, he traveled from Korea to Japan and studied Daito-aikijujitsu. The later founder

> **Hapkido possesses the deflectiveness associated with Aikido and also has the impact of Tae Kwon Do, but it is not the product of either.**

of Aikido, Morihei Uyeshiba, also studied at this school. This is generally where the wrongful link between the two martial arts are formulated.

Choi, upon returning to Korea, integrated the defensive mechanisms of the Japanese style including: the locking techniques, commonly associated with Jujutsu; the use of an opponent's own energy against himself, linked to modern Aikido; and the strong kicking and punching techniques of the Korean martial arts. Hapkido, therefore, possesses the deflectiveness associated with Aikido and also has the impact of Tae Kwon Do, but it is not the product of either.

Hapkido's initial element of defense is that of nonresistance. The first priority, in any confrontational situation, is to not allow an aggressor to grab or strike you. This is accomplished, quite easily, by simply stepping out of the way of the oncoming aggression, or by consciously diverting the opponent's limb away from your body

If, however, the aggressor continues to punch or kick, or does catch a hold of you, then, take that energy that he has used and divert it against him. Disengage his hold or deflect his strike and then perform a powerful counterattack with a kick

An attacker grabs you by the collar As he pulls you forward, you place your leg behind his, while striking him in his throat. The attacker falls to the ground.

The opponent launches a left punch at you. By leaning back, out of its way, it misses. A second, right-hand punch is attempted by the attacker; it is deflected. While the left arm checks the opponent's still extended right arm, a right knife-hand is delivered to his throat as he is thrown to the ground.

An assailant grabs you from behind. Pivoting, you turn, grab and lock his wrist. A knife-hand strike is made to the opponent's ribs. As the forward leg goes around his leg, the arm comes up to his neck level, strikes, and he is thrown to the ground.

If the aggressor continues to punch or kick, or does catch a hold of you, then, take that energy that he has used and divert it against him. Disengage his hold or deflect his strike and then perform a powerful counterattack with a kick or a hand technique to quickly end the confrontation.

or a hand technique to quickly end the confrontation.

One may question, how does non-resistance come into this apparent aggressive action? First of all, one must understand that non-resistance does not imply non-self-preservation. What it does imply, is that one should not meet an opponent on his level, eventually succeeding or losing blow to blow One should utilize a concise formula or method to overcome the opponent, expediently and to minimize possible injury to one's self.

Hapkido's Three Central Elements

Hapkido has three central elements which make up its theory of defense and offense. They are:

1) Deflection and use of an opponent's own aggressive energy against himself.

2) Continuous flowing movement from one technique on to the next.

3) Total penetration of an opponent's offense and defense.

By viewing each of these elements individually, we will come to a better understanding of why Hapkido's theory of defense and

79

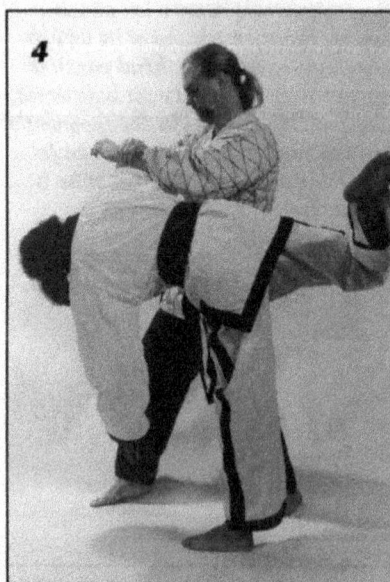

A straight punch is attempted by the attacker It is deflected, then his elbow is locked by your two arms coming up in opposite directions. The opponent's elbow can be broken at this point, as he are tossed to the ground.

artists know, blocking an attack straight on may cause damage to you yourself. Yes, the adversary's technique may be stopped, but the arm, or leg, that blocked it might be hurt in the process. Thus, one would have one less fully functional weapon to call upon if the confrontation continues.

A further illustration to comprehend this concept more clearly is to imagine an opponent who begins a straight punch at you. By simply side-stepping the attack and deflecting the fist, the opponent will continue to move forward due to his own momentum. Thus, his attack has been nullified. Then, continue through with a focused counterstrike with the leg or arm and the confrontation is over.

Continuation from one technique to the next is also elemental in Hapkido's theory of self-defense. For what is the purpose of simply deflecting an attacker's assault without additionally debilitating him so that he can not launch a further aggression upon you?

Further, according to Hapkido theory, a proper method of defense allows one to form a continuous flowing motion from one technique to the next — be they defensive or offensive. In this way, a continuum of energy may be focused by the Hapkido practitioner, thereby allowing minimal energy expenditure and maximum result. This is accomplished by having the ability to quickly change one's own positioning and defense strategy

An example of this continuous technique is found in the defense of an attacker's oncoming punch. The punch is diverted with a circular into-out deflection. The Hapkido technician then continues through, with a counterassault, by spinning his body around and delivering a backfist to the opponent's head.

The purpose of developing the ability to effortlessly flow from one technique to the next, is that one must never allow one's self to be so

offensive is so effective.

The deflection of an opponent's energy is based on "the law of forward motion." As illustrated above, by allowing the opponent's pulling of your collar to continue, no energy was expended on your part. You simply stepped behind his leg, as he pulled you towards himself. Not only was your own strike given added impact by this, but once he was struck, his fall was imminent.

To look at another example of deflection of an opponent's energy,

imagine a punch or a leg technique is launched at you. By deflecting its attack while allowing its motion to continue through, the opponent, inadvertently, continues to move forward with the force of his own power By re-directing an opponent's own energy, it becomes virtually an effortless form of self-defense.

According to Hapkido theory, the reason an attack should be deflected rather than met with a traditional block, is that, as all martial rigid that he is locked into the last technique that he has delivered. Why? Because, as one can never assume what the opponent may unleash, one should never be so bound by the previous technique to not be able to move quickly and easily onto another one which will facilitate the end of the confrontation more readily

By following this strategy it allows one to quickly change, re-focus, or redirect one's momentum and movements as specified by the particular confrontational situation.

The third and final point of the Hapkido theory of self-defense is total penetration of an opponent's offense and defense. This is accomplished not only through the use and manipulation of an adversary's own energy against himself, but the ability to strike first and fast inside of his defenses.

Squaring off with an opponent and allowing him to make the first move, that will probably be defended, is more descriptive of an old Western film than a competent self-defense strategy For this reason, if a hostile opponent is in front of you a debilitating front kick, or similar technique, will end the confrontation before it has the opportunity to begin.

The End Goal of Self-Defense

There is no purpose in the trading of blows with an opponent; leaving the stronger of the two surviving. Ultimately, the only goal of any confrontation is to walk away victorious, in one piece. This being accepted and understood, what must the martial artist do to achieve this goal?

Strike first, strike fast, before you can be injured, and strike with focused precision. To this end goal, Hapkido does not grab or strike at an opponent randomly It is necessary to make any successful defense, or assault, a targeted attack. For this reason, it is necessary for a person to understand the vulnerable pressure points on an individual.

Pressure and strike points are key common knowledge to all martial artists. The most elemental ones, are, of course: the throat, the temples, the nose, the eyes, the solar plexus and the knees. All strikes must find their way to one of these or other key points, or there is little use in them being preformed. For, to fight consciously, is to win. Impacts to non-elemental parts of the opponent's body may have the ability to ultimately take a toll on them. The con-

scious strike, however, ends the confrontation quickly

Close-Encounter Locking

Joint-locking, trapping and throwing techniques are commonly associated with Hapkido. The knowledge of these techniques expand further upon the focal strike zones of a martial artist. For once, one understands how an opponent's joints can be used against him. Not only can his aggressive attack energies be further redirected, but also the number of calculated impact points have increased greatly

The most rapid way to come to an understanding of how these joint-locking techniques are implemented, is to bend any of your own joints the wrong way Quickly, you will come to an understanding of how easy it is to control an adversary when the same technique is done to him.

Hapkido, though obviously a formulated self-defense system, comes down to a no-nonsense, no-holds-barred method of self-preservation. It is designed, as we have seen, to use an opponent's own aggressive actions against him — all to the defender's advantage.

So, aggressors beware when you encounter a practitioner of the martial arts who understands and practices the principles of Hapkido!■

Dr. Scott Shaw is a Hapkido/Tae Kwon Do stylist with 28 years of experience under his black belt. As an actor, he has starred in such features as The Roller Blade Seven; Samurai Vampire Bikers from Hell; The Atomic Samurai; *and was recently featured in Robert Altman's* The Player.

Lock 'em & Throw 'em

Hapkido Style

By Scott Shaw

An angered attacker attempting to intimidate you, comes up and grabs you by your shirt. A common reaction to this type of attack is to follow the aggressor's lead and grab a hold of him, as well. This type of defensive action generally only enrages your opponent further and escalates the confrontation to a grappling match which lands both of you on the ground, fighting like cats and dogs.

The second common alternative to someone grabbing a hold of you, is to strike him with either a punch or a kick. Though a precisely directed strike may prove to be more effective than the preceding counter attack, this type of very aggressive behavior may not always suit the environment or situation you find yourself in.

There is, however a simpler much more effective course of action a conscious martial artist may take to a grabbing attack. That method is to rapidly analyze what body joint of your opponent is exposed and accessible. Then, with precise joint locking technique, you can lock that joint, easily disengaging your opponent's grasp on you, and effortlessly throw him to the ground.

The techniques of locking elements of your opponent's body and then throwing him to the ground has become synonymous with the martial art system of Hapkido.

Hapkido's philosophy dictates that it is not necessary to meet force with force. Instead, it is far more effective to respond with a self defense strategy which your opponent would not expect and a counter attack which uses your opponent's own aggressive energy against himself. Joint locking gives you both: surprise advantage and easy control of the altercation.

To begin our study of Hapkido joint locking, simply take your hand and bend one of your fingers back in the direction it is not suppose to go. The obvious reaction to this is discomfort. Imagine the reaction you would obtain if you were to perform this finger bending technique, very aggressively, on an attacking opponent.

An opponent powerfully grabs your throat with one of his hands. You rapidly reach up to his grip. With your hand and

fingers, you dislodge one of his fingers from his grasp. Immediately, you rapidly and powerfully bend that finger back, towards him. Due to the pain you are inflicting on his finger he instantly releases his grasp on your neck. Thus, you are freed from his choke hold and you may have broken his finger in the process, depending on how powerfully you bent it back. Once you have a controlling hold of your opponent's finger you can easily dominate his motions by maintaining pressure on that finger or effortlessly throw him to the ground, by simply bending his finger back further towards his own arm and directing him in the direction of the ground.

Though the bending back of the finger is a very simplistic illustration, it is not only a very viable joint locking technique, as we have just seen, but is a very poignant example of how easy control over your opponent can be maintained by locking his joints; leaving him in a defensively inadequate position. Thus, he can not readily come back at you with further attack.

The key element, which makes all joint locks effective, is to move a joint in a direction it does not normally go. By manipulating a joint against itself, you invariably come to a superior degree of control over your opponent; much more so than you could obtain by simply struggling with him muscle to muscle.

Of course, many holds that an opponent grabs you with are not as easy to free yourself from, as the one previously described. This is why Hapkido teaches us that whenever we are grabbed, our initial reaction, prior to locking our opponent's joint, is to strike him in a pressure point first. These pressure point strike zones include, but are not limited

Above: (1) An attacker grabs your shirt. (2) You palm strike him under his nose to loosen his grasp. (3) Grabbing a hold of his thumb you powerfully bend it backwards, locking his wrist. (4) With the aid of your other hand, controlling his elbow, you throw him to the ground.

Below: (1) An attacker grabs your shoulder from the rear. (2) You take a hold of his hand and (3) lock his wrist.

to: the nose, throat, solar plexus, groin, and knees.

By striking your opponent, just before disengaging his hold with a joint lock, not only do you momentary distract him, possibly injuring him, but in the process he will loosen his grip just enough that it will be easier to end his hold on you and you will be able to lock whichever of his body joints you are attempting to control more easily.

The joint lock target on your opponent is dominated by what type of hold your opponent has on you. Virtually any joint on the human body can be locked and manipulated under the right placement and circumstances. The decision of which one to use, in a given situation, is largely dictated by how your opponent has taken a hold of you. For if a joint is not easily locked, it is not the one to focus on, as this will only prove to be a battle of individual strengths. Therefore, the key is to find a joint that is either already exposed or easy to take a hold of.

The wrist is a bodily joint that can be easily locked. To demonstrate an example of this to yourself, take your hand and push it in, towards your arm. You will no doubt feel the pressure and ultimate pain this causes. Now, reverse the shove and push your hand back away from your arm. Again, you will observe the discomfort. You can now clearly understand that when your opponent's wrist is taken control of, you can easily dominate and limit his aggressive actions.

An opponent grabs you by your shirt. You strike to a pressure point to disarm the strength of his hold. Now, take a hold of his grabbing hand, by placing your thumb on top of his hand near it's center and wrapping your fingers around his wrist. Powerfully, twist the hand over on top of itself and bend it in towards the opponent's arms, arching it slightly to one side. By joint locking your opponent's wrist in this way, his grasp on you is released and his hand and wrist joint are locked; not doubt causing him pain. From this superior positioning you have substantial control over his movements. You can add more pressure to the hold if additional control is necessary, or if you desire, by twisting the wrist further you can throw your opponent to the ground.

One of the main things to consider before you attempt to joint lock any bodily part on your opponent, is to decide beforehand if you will have to fight, muscle to muscle with him, to take control. If you will have to, this is not the joint to attempt to lock, for this type of strength vs. strength defense is

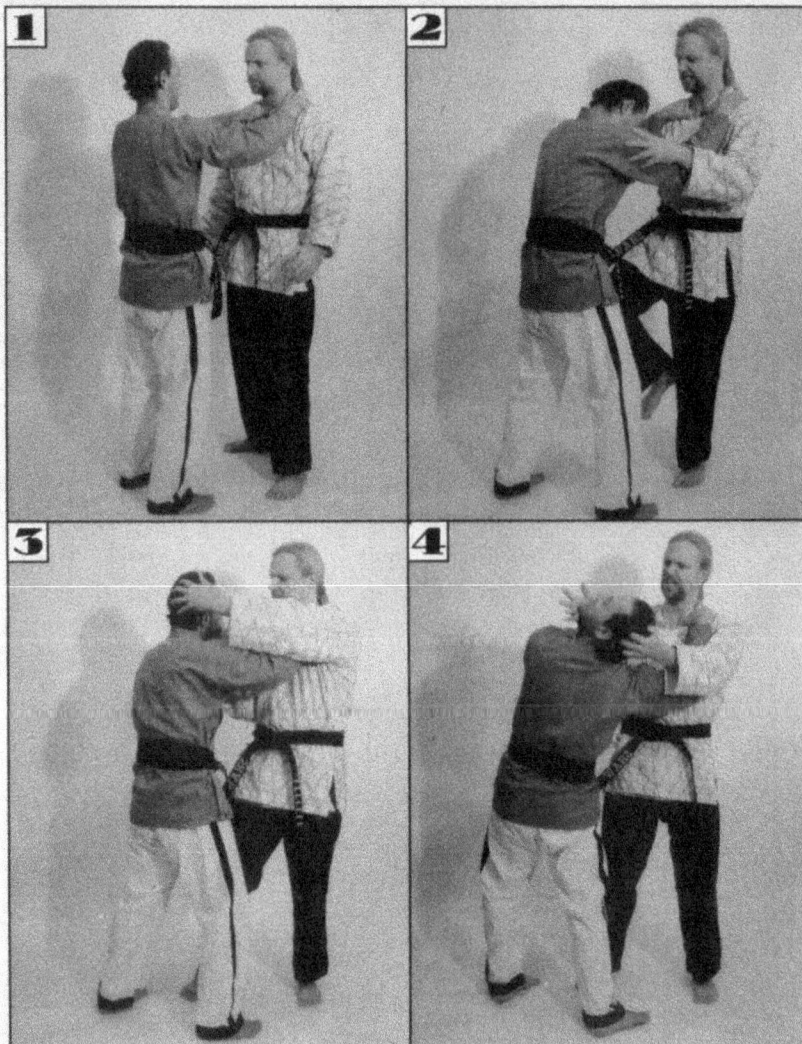

(1) You are grabbed in a two handed choke hold. (2) You knee your opponent in the groin. (3) Reaching in you twist and lock his neck. (4) From here, he can be easily thrown to the ground.

"An opponent grabs you by your shirt. You strike to a pressure point to disarm the strength of his hold."

86

(1) An opponent grabs you in front with one of his arms. (2) By bring your arm up and over his, (3) then underneath, you lock his elbow. (4) With a sweep kick, as you lift at his locked elbow up, he is sent backwards to the ground.

"The neck is an easily manipulated joint lock target."

virtually the same as attempting to wrestle his grip free with traditional yanking and pulling methods and is to no one's advantage. The joint you should aim for is one you know you will be able to effortlessly control.

Joint lock theory teaches us to view the positioning of our body in proportion to that of our opponent, and then lock the joint on his body which is most easy to grip and manipulate, in relation to where we are currently located. For example, your opponent has grabbed you in a two handed choke hold around your neck. You first loosen his grasp by punching him in the solar plexus or kneeing him in the groin. You then, instantly reach in, twisting his neck to one side, slightly upward, with both of your hands. Then, by pivoting his body away from yours and downward, you effortlessly throw him to the ground.

As we have just seen, because our opponent was standing directly in front of us, one of the easiest joints of his body to manipulate was his neck. Therefore, we reached in and controlled it and did not have to fight to manipulate it in the direction we desired.

The neck is an easily manipulated joint lock target. This is because the neck's muscle structure does not possess a strong ability to fend off a well placed single or double hand grab which will shove it to either side. Once the neck is pushed sideways, past its natural limit, the spine is instantly locked and there is little your opponent can easily do to retreat from this hold. Therefore, from superior positioning, manipulation of your opponent becomes quite easy.

The elbow is another of the primary focal points of effective joint locking. This is due to the fact, that when an opponent grabs a hold of your clothing or body, there is generally a certain distance between his body and yours. This distance is bridged by his arm, with his elbow at the center generally remaining very exposed.

The type of joint manipulation you can unleash on your opponent's elbow is as simple as powerfully striking downward on top of it with a knife hand. This will not only loosen but perhaps disengage your opponent's grip on you altogether. If you leave this knife hand strike in place and instantly bend his forearm back onto itself by using your other hand, you can easily maintain control over your standing opponent or rapidly send him to the ground simply by pivoting around, as you direct his body downward.

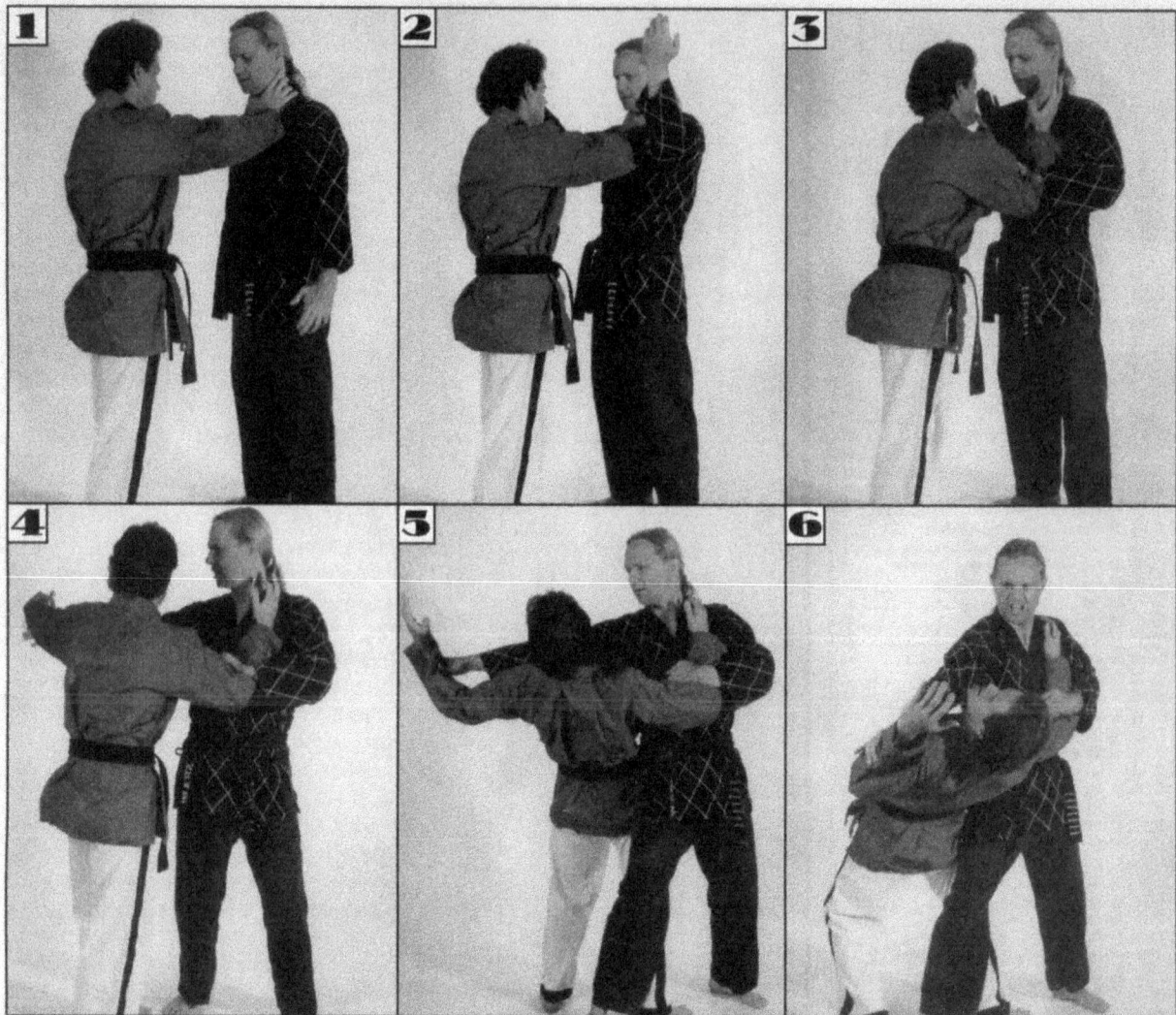

(1) You are grabbed with a two handed front choke hold. (2) You bring knife hands into your opponent's elbow joint, (3) dislodging his grasp. (4) Leaving one knife hand in place, to maintain control, (5) you throw your opponent to the ground by guiding his other arm out (6) and around him.

More advanced elbow joint locking can be put into action when your opponent grabs a hold of you with one arm. This is accomplished by extending your arm up and over his grabbing arm and then powerfully lifting your arm up, underneath his elbow joint. Due to his grab, his elbow is locked. Even if he releases his grasp, you still maintain control over his motion because his grabbing hand is forced under your arm pit and thus his hand, elbow and arm are completely locked into place. You can hold him in this elbow lock, or if you prefer by continuing through with additional force on his elbow you can lift it up further as you sweep kick him. He will be easily sent to the ground.

Joint locking is ideally suited to disengage opponent's body grabs on you, as we have witnessed. But, joint locking, leading to throws, is equally

"**More advanced elbow joint locking can be put into action when your opponent grabs a hold of you with one arm.**"

88

effective for punching assaults, as well. For example, your opponent punches at you. You side step the attack, while deflecting his arm, with an in-to-out knife hand block, just behind his elbow. You then rapidly lock his elbow by bringing your other arm up and in against the inside of his forearm. With your two arms in place, his elbow is now locked. You can choose to maintain control over him from this joint lock or continue through, pivoting and throwing him forcefully to the ground.

As we have seen, Hapkido's joint locking theory not only makes freeing yourself from an opponent's grabs virtually effortless, but it takes the reliance on strength out of your self defense method. By putting joint lock theory into practice, you learn to control your opponent with minimal energy thereby making your victory in any physical confrontation quick, quiet, and precise.

(1) Your attacker punches. (2) By side stepping and deflecting the punch, with a knife hand block, and then, (3) simultaneously, bringing your other arm up and in, (4) you lock your opponent's elbow joint. (5) By pivoting, he is easily sent to the ground.

89

Hapkido Joint Locks for Self Defense

These techniques, when mastered, can be dramatically effective and excruciatingly painful.

By Scott Shaw

As evolving martial artists, we all understand, for each type of fighting situation you find yourself, there is the most appropriate method of defense to deal with each individual manner of attack. The type of defensive application you put to use is largely dominated by the method of attack your opponent has launched at you, and perhaps more importantly, the overall intention of his attack.

For example, if your opponent comes at you with a very forceful punching and kicking offense, then to save yourself from immediate injury, you must defend your body with very aggressive methods. On the other hand, if the altercation you find yourself in is at its inception, and your opponent has simply grabbed a part of your body or a piece of your clothing, in order to intimidate you, it would not only be unnecessary to counter attack with extremely aggressive methods but an over reactive waste of energy, as well.

At its most elementary level, the Korean martial art of Hapkido teaches its practitioners, "You should never expend more energy than is absolutely necessary to successfully defend yourself." This is to say, in the case of a grabbing attack, you should not amplify a confrontation which is in progress, by forcefully attempting to pull away from a grabbing opponent and then relocating your position and entering into a fighting stance. The reason this is not a sound defensive measure is because, from this aggressive posturing, your attacking opponent and yourself will then have to go head to head into an unpredictable battle. It is Hapkido's defensive belief, it is a far more efficient means of defending yourself, to instead, immediately take action from the exact point of the altercations inception. In this way, you will not only have the rapid counter attack surprise advantage, but you will not alert your opponent to the fact you are intending to defend yourself.

As this imaginary confrontation has begun by your opponent simply grabbing a hold of a part of your body or clothing, to launch into an overzealous aggressive counter attack would not only be uncalled for but unnecessary, as well. To this end, when you face this type of confrontational situation, it is to your advantage to find a much more expedient method of dealing with the attack. This is the ideal circumstance to put a Hapkido joint lock into action. By immediately joint locking your opponent into submission, instead of fighting him, blow by blow, he will not have the ability to continue his attack any further on you and the confrontation will come to an abrupt halt.

Hapkido, begins by teaching its elementary students joint locking techniques from an opponent's wrist grab attack. This is because defending against the wrist grab is a great teaching element.

The wrist grab is a very effective grasp to learn how to first, effectively break free from and then turn that disengaging technique into an effective joint lock. The Hapkido disengaging techniques and joint locks learned from the wrist grab applications can later be altered as necessary to use against more destructive types of grabbing attacks.

Hapkido wrist grab techniques, are defined in two ways: Straight Arm Grab and Cross Arm Grab. The Straight Arm Grab implies you are standing face to face with your opponent and he grabs your wrist with his opposite arm; i.e.. his left arm to your right arm. Cross Arm Grab defines a grab which reaches across your opponent's body; example: his right arm to your right arm.

An opponent has Straight Arm grabbed a hold of you by your wrist. A common and spontaneous type of defense would be attempting to recklessly pull free from this attack. Though this is a natural response, it is highly ineffective. Even if you do achieve your freedom, your opponent, having the attacking advantage, will instantly continue his aggressive assault on you. Therefore, to effectively solve the problem of this Straight Arm wrist grabbing attack, instead of randomly attempt-

Photographs by Hae Won Shin

1

Your opponent grabs your wrist in Straight Arm fashion.

2

By pivoting the palm of your hand upwards, you lightly lock your opponent's wrist.

3

With the aid of your free hand, you take control of his hand, and powerful lock his wrist.

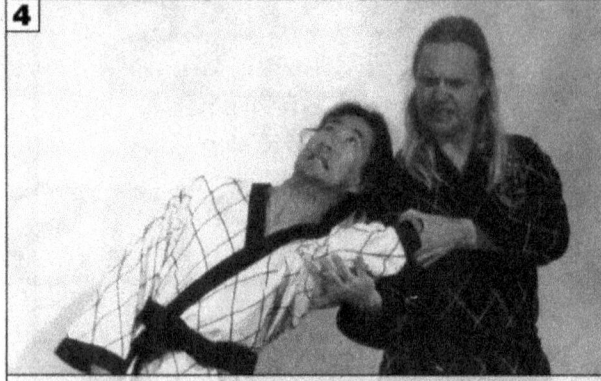

4

Now, that your hand is free, you use it to shove up on his elbow, while putting pressure downwards on his wrist. Thus, locking his entire arm.

You are grabbed at wrist level in Cross Arm fashion (1). You pivot your hand down, under, and around your opponent's grasp (2). At the same time, you apply a knife hand strike to his elbow (3). By continuing through with knife hand pressure to his elbow, while his wrist is held, you lock his arm (4).

ing to pull free, Hapkido teaches, "The first step in any joint lock defense is to disengage your opponent's controlling grasp on you."

This is accomplished in one of two ways. The first method is, "Rapidly move the grabbed element of your body in a direction your opponent can not maintain his grip." The second method is to "Shift the direction of your adversary's grasp to your own advantage." In either case, once the initial opponent's grasp has been dislocated, is when you actually lock his joint.

In the case of the Straight Arm wrist grab, if you chose to first, properly disengage your opponent's hold on you, this can be successfully achieved by simultaneously pivoting your body in the direction away from your opponent, as you drive your arm out, forward, and away from your opponent in a linear fashion. This is most ideally achieved by first forming your hand in Knife Hand fashion; thus, tensing the muscles and tendons of your hand and wrist. As you are rapidly pulling away from your opponent's grasp, in a direction his hand will not have the ability to maintain a hold on you, you instantly free yourself.

Freedom is generally not enough to gain victory in these types of confrontations. You must instantly move forward with a defensive action which will render your opponent helpless in launching an further attacks on you.

Hapkido practices "Continual Motion Theory," this is to say, you should not break up your defensive techniques into several distinct and separate motions. Instead, it is far more effective, in a combative situation, if your defensive techniques easily and effortlessly flow from one onto the next.

In the case of the previously described Straight Arm freeing exercise, you can gain instant, substantial control over your opponent, if, while you are pivoting and pulling free from his wrist grab, you take control of his grasping hand with your free hand at the moment you begin your pivot to freedom. This is easily accomplished by grabbing your fingers to the inside of his palm, as your thumb grabs the outer part of his hand.

Now, that you have freed yourself and taken control of your opponent's hand, you can simply, rapidly guide his arm under your shoulder as you pivot free from his grasp. By lifting your shoulder up at your opponent's elbow region, his elbow will become instantly locked and you have taken control of the budding confrontation.

As we have seen, by following the path of least resistance, while putting to use Hapkido's "Continuous Motion Theory" you have freed yourself from an attacking opponent and have instantaneously gained joint locking control over his actions.

Another very effective joint locking method for the Straight Arm grab, is to put the second of Hapkido's joint lock principal into use, that of, "Shifting the direction of your adversary's grasp to your own advantage."

Your opponent Straight Arm grabs you. Simply by pivoting your grabbed wrist to an upward facing position, you begin the joint locking process on your opponent, as his grabbing wrist has now been arched to an unnatural position. Now, with the palm of your grabbed hand facing upward, you take a hold of your opponent's gripping hand with your free hand, by placing your thumb to the back of his hand and your finger inside of his palm. You now can effectively arch and lock his wrist back farther To add even further control, your now freed hand takes a hold of him at his elbow and then by pushing upwards you have gained total control of his motion.

In the case of an opponent's Cross Arm grab, you can use the second in Hapkido's joint locking principals, as well.

Your opponent has Cross Arm grabbed a hold of your wrist. First, step slightly outside of this face to face encounter to add leverage to what you will do next. Now, by pivoting your grabbed hand outside, up and, over his grasp, you begin to lock his wrist. At the same time, you can deliver a Knife Hand strike to the outside elbow of his grabbing arm. By doing this, you gain additional control over the confrontation.

By allowing the knife hand strike to stay in place at your opponent's outer elbow and by rolling it over as you take a hold of his grabbing wrist, you have instantly changed the tides of this grabbing attack. You now hold him joint locked by maintaining a pulling back hold on his arm, while keeping his elbow locked with your Knife Hand maintaining downward pressure. This technique will even break the opponent's elbow, in extreme conditions.

Certainly Hapkido does not limit its joint locking prowess to the wrist grab. The same techniques you just learned can be expanded upon and put to use in other situations.

Your opponent takes a hold of you by the front of your shirt. By simply reaching over his hand and grasping it, with your thumb to the back of it, your fingers on his palm, (as we learned in the first exercise), you can rapidly bend it back over itself, instantly locking it. Now, by combining this technique with the second one we learned, (pressure to the elbow), you can continue forward and lock both his hand and elbow and hold him into a position where he can not cause you any more problems.

Hapkido joint locks were developed in fashion that they may be utilized as your defensive situation dictates. Though a specific joint locking technique may illustrate an opponent's elbow joint being locked once he has grabbed onto your shoulder, this same technique may be effectively executed when the opponent has single-handedly grabbed you by your throat. Therefore, The key element to remember when learning and then putting Hapkido joint locks to use is they can be used to defend against numerous types of attacks. Their individual effectiveness is only dominated by your ability to disengage your opponent's grasp on you and lock his joints appropriately. ◄

Being forcefully grabbed from behind by an attacker is one of the most serious situations even the most trained martial artist will ever face. If an attacker grabs you from behind, you are not only instantly thrown off balance, but your attacker has an enormous amount of control over any movements you may attempt to make. What then can the conscious martial artist do to turn the tides of advantage away from the attacker when taken a hold of from behind? To understand what is best done in combating a rear attack, we must first view some elemental rules.

First of all, if you are forcefully grabbed from the rear recklessly attempting to forcefully free yourself from the hold by pulling

Many people, when grabbed from behind, immediately attempt to turn and face their opponent. Though this is the natural instinct and of course by facing your opponent you expect to be in a better position to defend yourself. This, however, is not always the case when initially grabbed from behind. For if your opponent already has a hold on you, by recklessly turning into him at close range, you open yourself up to be powerfully hit by him as you struggle to achieve this positioning. Therefore, this is not the prescribed course of action either

Now that we understand what not to do, let us examine some methods which will greatly enhance your defense situation if you are ever grabbed from behind.

defensive movement and begin to take appropriate action the moment you are grabbed from the rear By allowing any time to elapse will only allow your opponent to strengthen his hold on you. As seconds progress in this defensive posture, his ability to dominate the confrontation will increase and yours will decrease.

Therefore, the moment you are grabbed from behind, you should subscribe to another Hapkido rule of thumb, "Immediately strike your opponent before you follow through with any additional defensive action." By doing this, you not only will substantially loosen any grasp your opponent has on you, but will stun him, hopefully, long enough that further defensive action can be taken on your part.

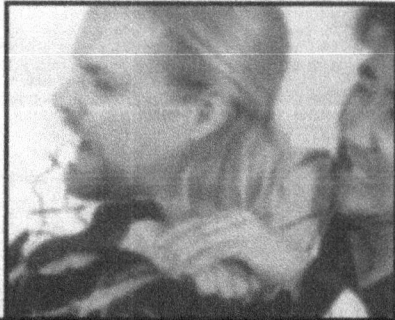

Grabbed From

and jerking serves little purpose. As your attacker has no doubt taken a firm hold on you, the strength of his grasp will only increase by your randomly fighting to free yourself. Additionally, as he has a superior rear grasp on you, by aimlessly fighting, he may simply change his mode of attack and begin to deliver severe blows to the back of your head or your kidneys. Therefore, recklessly fighting to free yourself from a rear attack is never in your best interest.

In the Korean martial art of Hapkido, it is understood that, "No defensive movement should ever be made unless it will have a substantially debilitating effect on your attacking opponent." In other words, do nothing which will waste your energy! It is also understood, on the other hand, "You must always immediately take appropriate action, the moment an attack is launched upon you."

In the rear grab situation, you must immediately shift your mind set into serious

Say, for example, your opponent has grabbed you by the shoulder and is pulling you back with one hand. Instead of allowing his grab to control your motion and possibly send you backwards to the ground, you should immediately realign your footing by stepping back, towards him. By doing this, even though his grasp on you still remains, you will at least have competent footing.

Immediately upon realignment of your footing, you must move into an offensive

94

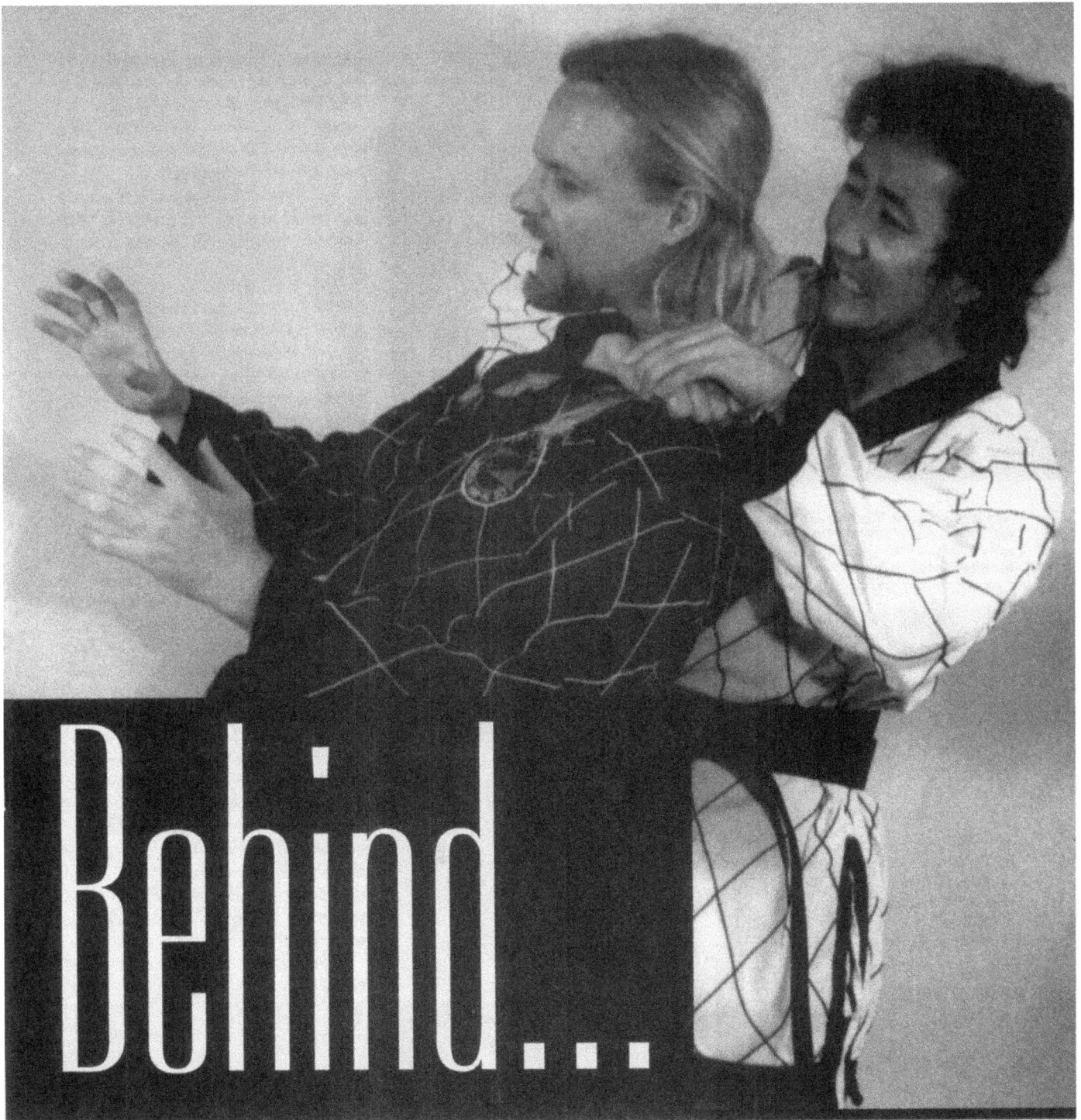

Behind....

Being forcefully grabbed from behind by an attacker is one of the most serious situations even the most trained martial artist will ever face.

By Scott Shaw

An opponent two hand grabs you and pulls you backwards from behind (1). You allow his force to pull you back, as you step behind his leg, gaining balance (2). You pivot and lock your arm down, under, and around one of his grabbing arms (3), as you palm strike him to his nose (4). Your other palm goes to the back of his shoulder. You propel him forward, throwing him to the ground (5).

posture and strike your opponent. As he has pulled you back, towards him, this initial strike may well be actualized by pivoting towards him, on your now stable leg, and striking him with an elbow or a knife hand strike to his temples.

By allowing the force of his backward pull on you define what type of defense strike you make, you not only gain speed in your reaction but gain additional power due to the fact the forced movement towards him has already been instigated by his energy pulling you backwards. Therefore, as per Hapkido defensive guidelines, you have not wasted any of your own energy in initially moving to break free from the grip, instead you have taken advantage of his own pulling energy to move you in towards him and have simply struck him with your most easily available weapon.

Once you have made this initial strike, you must follow forward with another of Hapkido's primary principals, that of, "Continual Motion." This principal instructs us that we must immediately follow one technique with the next. For if you do not immediately follow up your initial strike with additional techniques, your opponent will no doubt unleash additional aggressive techniques upon you.

In the case of being pulled backwards by your opponent, and then striking him to his temple, by following the "Continual Motion Theory," you will then want to immediately strike him with additional techniques, to keep him from striking at you. Once these strikes have been accomplished, you must debilitate him to the degree that he will not have the opportunity to eventually come back at you. For this reason, Hapkido often will throw an opponent to the ground.

In the case of the previous described rear grab, by continuing further through

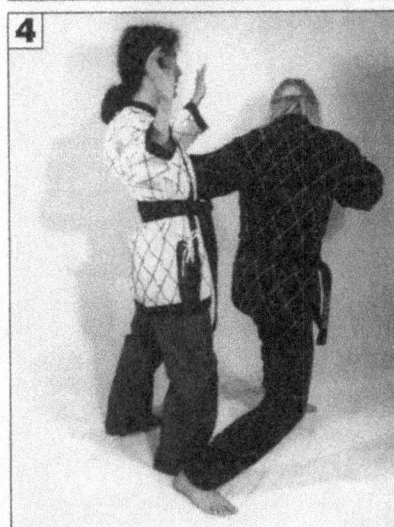

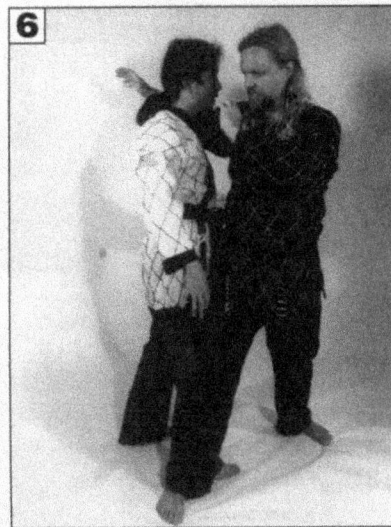

with your pivot to the rear, you can effortlessly lock your arm under and then over your opponents grabbing arm, at his shoulder level. Again, these continual movements are all performed instantaneously, thus your opponent will, no doubt, still have a hold on your back. Once his arm is locked, you can easily send him to the ground by taking a hold of the locking arm's wrist and moving it forward and downward in a continuing direction.

At times, simply the force and energy of your opponent, expending in his rear grab on you is all you will need to place yourself in the appropriate situation to defend yourself. For example, if your opponent has taken a hold of you and is pulling Logo backwards at your shoulder level with both of his hands; you can easily move backwards with the energy of his attack, waiting until the appropriate moment of action.

To defend yourself in this waiting fashion, you must first and foremost remain very

An attacker two arm grabs you from behind, restraining your arms down to your side (1). You extend your arms up and out at chest level (2). You immediately deliver several elbow strikes to your opponent (3-5). You lock your arm around his neck and throw him to the ground (6-8).

97

conscious of your footing. Then, by waiting for the appropriate moment when his backward pulling force has reached its pinnacle, you rapidly step one of your feet behind your opponent's legs. This will instantly stop his backward pulling motion on you. At this crux of position, rapidly pivot your body and lock your arm down under and around one of his grabbing arms, just as we discussed in the previous example, and then immediately grab a hold of your own wrist. From here, you can immediately throw him to the ground, thus ending this segment of the confrontation.

"If your arms are locked down, how then can you effectively strike or defend yourself?"

Not all rear grabs are as easily defended against as the previously described cases. Often times, an attacker will forcefully take hold of your entire body from the rear locking your arms down to your side. If your arms are locked down, how then can you effectively strike or defend yourself?

As your opponent will have grasped you in this position either by interlocking his fingers or by grabbing a hold of one of his own wrists, his grasp, no matter the strength, not have much lasting power. Therefore, by first of all slightly stepping back with one of your legs, allowing yourself stronger footing, you should rapidly thrust your arms forward and out at your chest level. This is not accomplished so much by brute strength, but it is achieved by a controlled internal energy. As you thrust your arms forward, his hold will easily be broken.

Once his hold has been disengaged, again, you must take immediate action to take control of the confrontation. This can be most readily accomplished by pivoting your body and delivering several elbow strikes into him, while allowing your back to remain facing him.

By leaving your back to him, your opponent will not have the ability to strike back at you to sensitive regions on your body, such as your race or your groin. Additionally, by leaving your back to him, you have utilized the least amount of your own personal energy in defending yourself.

Once you have debilitated your opponent with several elbow strikes to various points on his body, you can then pivot back, slightly farther, and take a powerful hold on his neck. Since you have achieved this hold, simply by pivoting through you effortlessly throw him to the ground where additional strikes can be delivered, if necessary.

No doubt one of the most serious types of rear grabs is when your opponent attacks you with a rear choke hold. Not only is the force of this grab very dangerous but it must be disengaged immediately before it has the ability to critically injure you.

The first step must be, the moment this type of attack occurs on you, is to, as discussed, instantly strike your opponent. This can be most quickly and debilitatingly accomplished by powerfully elbowing him to his ribs. From here, once his grasp is lessened, you must immediately take further action. This can be accomplished with additional elbow strikes to his body.

Once he has been suitably disabled, you can reach your arm up and around his neck, locking it into position. From here, he can be easily thrown over your forward leg, to the ground.

As we now understand, rear grabs do not have to be dealt with by randomly struggling with an opponent. Instead, if we keeps our wits about ourselves, they are effectively dealt with through the conscious use of "Continual Motion."

PHOTOS BY JOEL CINERO

MAKE THE GROUND YOUR ALLY

Hapkido Ground-Fighting Techniques

by Dr. Scott Shaw

You've been knocked down, you slipped or you were thrown while attempting a flamboyant kicking technique. Regardless of how it happened, you are on the ground looking up at your opponent. This does not mean, however, that you've lost and the fight is over

The key mistake many martial artists make while on the ground is to get up immediately Though this may be the natural response, it is usually not the best response. Not only does it give your opponent a better opportunity to strike you, but you can't defend yourself because you are probably using most of your limbs to stand up. To be sure, the ground is not the most advantageous fighting position to be in, but any situation is what you make of it. Therefore, what do you do?

In the Korean martial art *hapkido,* the following principles can be used in any combat situation:
1. Deflection and use of an opponent's own energy against himself.
2. Continuous flowing movement from one technique to the next.
3. Total penetration of an opponent's offenses and defenses.

Using these principles, you could handle an opponent's attack effectively When you are on the ground, your opponent will probably try to kick you. To prevent damage to your body that would adversely affect your fighting ability, respond with a technique from the first principle, which means you should block or deflect his attack and use his energy against himself. This is accomplished quite easily If your opponent is preparing to execute a front kick, block his kick with your forearm.

The second principle states that your movements should flow continuously from one technique to the next. Therefore, to prevent an injury to the body part you are blocking with, use a different technique to stop other attacks. For example, you can trap or lock your opponent's leg. To do this, place your blocking arm across your opponent's shin for leverage. With your other hand,

101

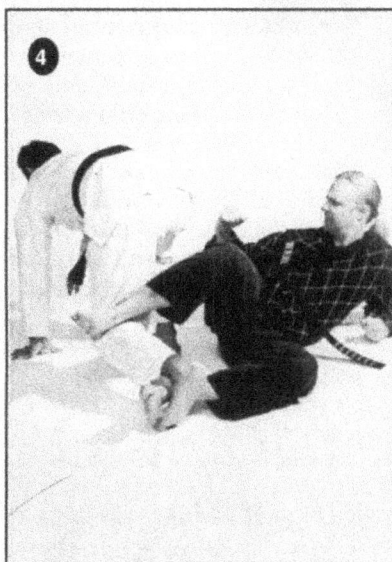

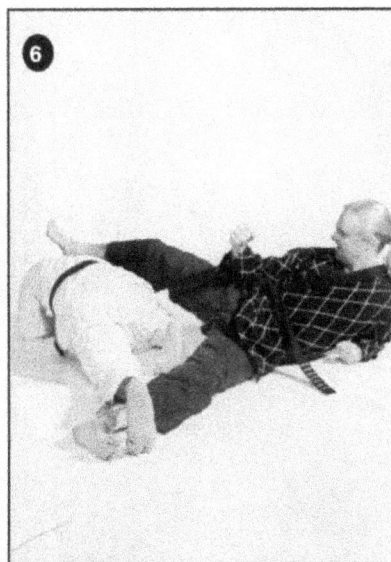

When you have been knocked down, the natural response is to get up. This, however, is not always the best response. In the above sequence, Scott Shaw (right) demonstrates (1) one effective technique. As his opponent attempts a side kick, Shaw, a hapkido stylist, blocks (2) the kick with his forearm and locks his adversary's leg at ankle level. With his other leg, Shaw strikes (3) his attacker behind the knee of his rear leg, causing (4) his opponent to fall. The hapkido stylist then raises (5) his right leg to execute a heel kick to his opponent's head, and he executes (6) the kick.

If you somehow end up on the ground, however, defense is not your only alternative.

grab your opponent's kicking leg behind his ankle. To knock him down, pull his leg up and shove him back with your blocking arm.

The biggest mistake martial artists can make is to think the confrontation is over after the opponent is thrown or trapped. It has been repeatedly proven in street fights that this is not the case. Besides, what is the point of throwing your opponent to the ground if you do not take advantage of this? Once he is down, execute a counterattack, which is the third principle.

This is the difference between hapkido and its distant relative *aikido*. In modern hapkido, any defensive maneuver must be followed with a powerful offensive maneuver to neutralize your opponent and end the confrontation. Aikido, on the other hand, is strictly a defensive art.

In accordance with hapkido's third principle, the counterattack is always delivered from the most optimum location. In ground fighting, the quickest counterattack would be delivered from the ground.

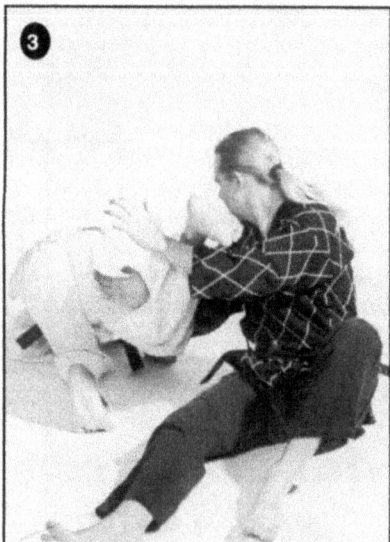

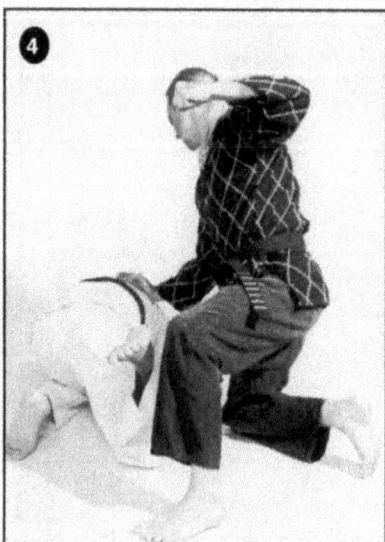

It's important to stay composed if you are knocked to the ground. In the sequence above, hapkido stylist Scott Shaw (right) holds (1) his hands in front of his face for protection while his opponent prepares to strike. When his adversary attempts a front kick, Shaw blocks (2) the kick with his forearm and grabs his adversary's ankle. Shaw then uses his upper hand to lock (3) his opponent's knee while forcefully pivoting his leg, knocking him down. Shaw scrambles up (4) and throws a punch to his fallen opponent's head.

Thus, performing a quick heel kick or rolling toward your opponent and punching him in the head are both effective maneuvers.

To better comprehend hapkido's ground-fighting theory, it is helpful to understand hapkido's range theory, which is a two-fold process. The first part deals with evaluating the distance between you and your opponent and deciding if you should move to enhance your effectiveness. You must determine whether you should move to another location to improve your strik-ing potential and ability to defend yourself, or whether you should stay where you are because of the possible negative effects of moving. Your options are dictated by your location much more when fighting on the ground than when fighting while standing.

Once you have decided to move or stay, you must work within the confines of your location and perform the most appropriate and effective techniques available. Knowing your response distance—the second part of the range theory—is one of the ultimate defensive keys to hapkido's fighting strategy To decide what defensive or offensive techniques would be most effective, you must evaluate your location, judge the distance between you and your opponent, and know what techniques will work effectively within this range. Since a common mistake martial artists make is to incorrectly assume that one technique works in every situation, hapkido's range theory analyzes the above elements to help practitioners understand what technique will work and why it will be effective in each situation.

Although your location limits the amount of joint locks you can perform while ground fighting, there are other effective techniques available. When your opponent is kicking you, use your forearm to block his kick and place your other hand on his ankle. Move your blocking hand around his knee and shove it forward. With your other hand, push backward against your opponent's foot. This will twist his leg

The biggest mistake martial artists can make is to think the confrontation is over after the opponent is thrown or trapped.

and knock him to the ground, face first. Follow up with an appropriate counterattack.

Modern hapkido has blended all of *tae kwon do's* elaborate footwork into its fighting arsenal. As a result, it is possible to not only block with your feet, but also to lock your opponent and throw him to the

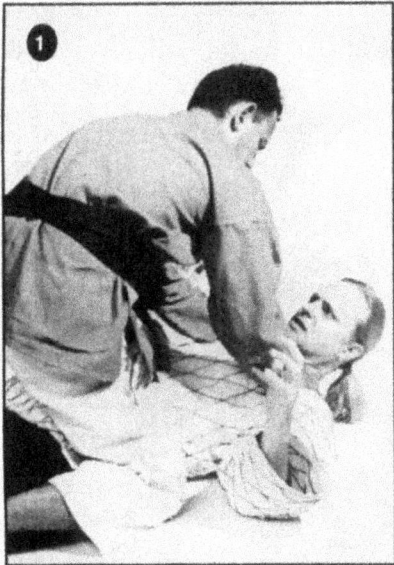
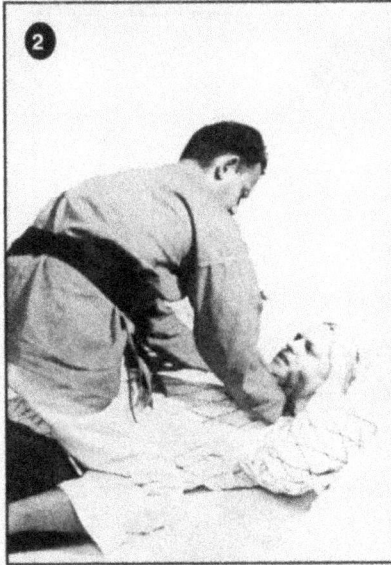
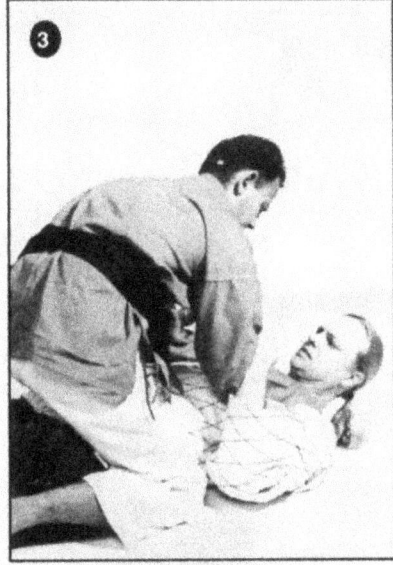
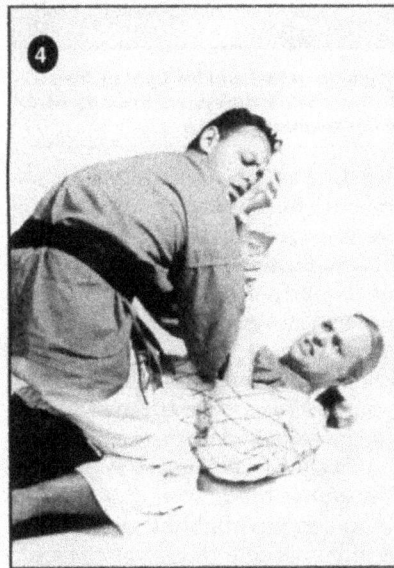
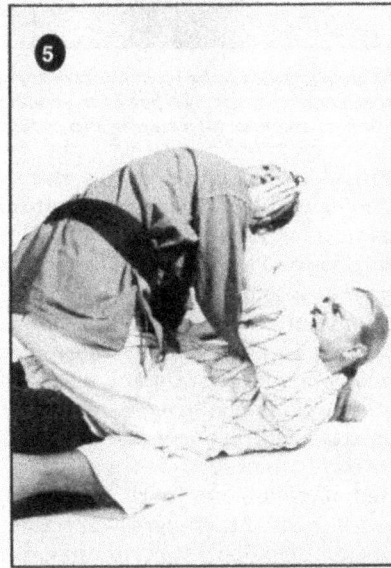
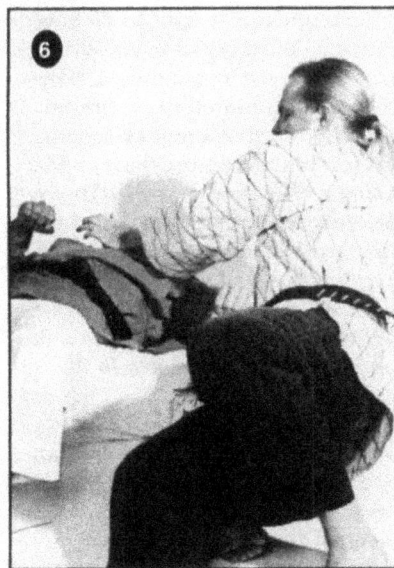
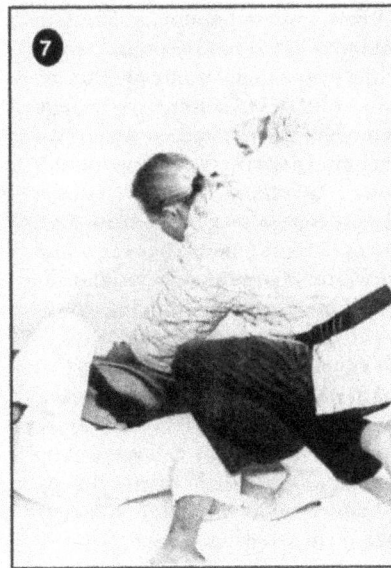

When you are on the ground, you have to be prepared for anything. In the sequence at the left, Scott Shaw (right) is faced (1) with an opponent who has jumped on top of him. While his opponent is choking him, Shaw raises (2) both of his hands and strikes (3) his adversary's elbow joints with knife hands. Shaw then executes (4) a palm strike to his opponent's face, twists (5) his head and throws (6) his opponent off. When his opponent is down, Shaw counters (7) with a punch.

ground with your legs. The foot-to-leg blocks are quite elemental. By intercepting your opponent's kick with a side kick, you have stopped its power

Locking your opponent's leg and throwing him down is another good technique. To do this, place one of your legs behind his leg, near his ankle. Snap your other leg quickly into a higher position in front of his leg. In a collapsing scissor-kick type motion, bring your legs together, causing your opponent to fall. Follow up with an appropriate counterattack.

Though many martial arts systems teach students how to execute various techniques, including sweeps, kicks and leg locks from the ground, these maneuvers are inadvisable. Knowledgeable street fighters or ring competitors know you should never go down on the ground willingly It is imprudent to place yourself in a less-than-optimum position to fight, because you can never be sure what your opponent's next offensive technique

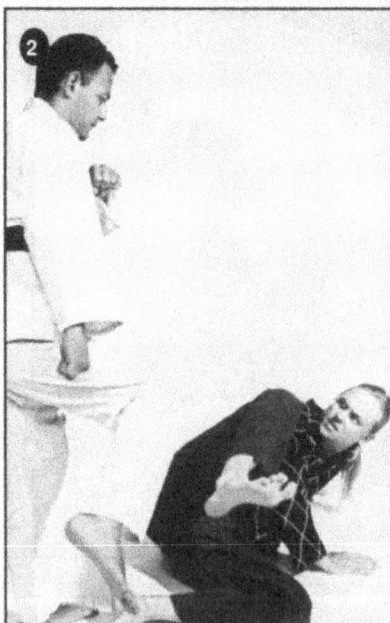

The ground may not be the most advantageous fighting position to be in, but it does not mean you have lost and the fight is over. Any situation is what you make of it. In the above sequence, Scott Shaw has been knocked (1) down. While his opponent prepares to deliver (2) a roundhouse kick, Shaw raises himself up and fires (3) a side kick to his opponent's midsection.

will be. Moreover, if your attack misses, then you are left in an undesirable location.

If you somehow end up on the ground, however, defense is not your only alternative. At times, the best defense may be an offense. If you raise your body off the ground with your arms to give you more force, you can easily execute a side kick to your opponent's knee or midsection. Afterward, you can stand up, especially since your opponent has been knocked backward, and you can take control of the fight.

The most dangerous situation you can find yourself in on the ground occurs when your opponent tries to jump on you to inflict further injury There are, however, several techniques you can use to overcome him. To begin with, it is important to make every move an offensive maneuver Do not waste any energy attempting to shove your attacker off you, because that is rarely successful. Without directed force and properly aimed counterattacks, the aggressor will maintain his superior positioning.

What can you do? Before you try to throw your opponent, strike one or more of his pressure points, such as his eyes, nose, solar plexus or elbow joints. Of course, your legs are powerful weapons, and you can use them to strike your opponent's groin. It's important to execute a strike before you try to manipulate your opponent's body, because this stuns him momentarily and a direct hit may cause him enough pain that it enables you to get away

If you disable your opponent with your strike, immediately throw him off you. The most effective way to do this is to grab the hair on the back of his head. While twisting his head away from you, place your other arm at shoulder level and

shove him off. If your opponent's hair is not long enough to grab and there is no article of clothing suitable to replace this grab zone, there is an equally effective method to remove an opponent. To begin with, grab his wrist and quickly shove his arm away from you. In a sweeping motion, use your other arm to strike his other wrist. You can now easily twist your adversary over and get on top of him.

In any ground fighting situation, it is imperative to try various techniques until one of them is successful. Remember, a specific technique will not be effective in every situation with every opponent. Therefore, to be completely prepared, practice with a trained opponent. Once you understand various applications, you can use them effectively on the street. No one likes to end up on the ground, but you can't always prevent it. If you find yourself on the ground, don't give up. If you keep your thoughts clear and do not panic, you can be victorious. ∎

About the Author· Dr Scott Shaw, who has a doctorate in Asian Studies, is a Hermosa Beach, California-based martial artist, actor and freelance writer

Hapkido Grappling Techniques

An enraged attacker grabs your shoulder. As you turn to face him, he flings his body at you, the two of you topple to the ground, and your assailant lands on top of you. You find yourself looking up at his fists as they bear down on you.

This type of ground-fighting situation occurs more frequently than you might think, even to trained martial artists. This is because, on the street, none of the traditional rules observed in the martial art studio or tournament ring apply. On the street, your opponent will no doubt strike at you with every weapon available to him. Martial artists must therefore learn how to defend themselves in an "anything-goes" type of grappling situation.

The mistake most people make when they find themselves on the bottom end of a grappling encounter is to attempt to haphazardly punch at an opponent who has the upper position. This type of defense serves little purpose. Not only will your opponent maintain his superior position, but his attack will be much more powerful than anything you can muster from the ground.

A second mistake many people make is to attempt to recklessly wiggle their way out from underneath their opponent once they find themselves on the ground. This type of unfocused grappling is a waste of energy. Your opponent will continue to inflict damage from his superior vantage point.

So what *should* you do when you find yourself in a ground-level grappling situation?

You must first free yourself, then disable your opponent so he cannot continue his attack.

The Korean martial art *hapkido* includes four rules to help practitioners emerge victorious in a grappling encounter:

• Never initiate your defense while in an inadequate position.

• Use your opponent's random, undirected energy to place yourself in a superior combat position.

• Anticipate your opponent's actions and use his energy against him.

• Never block when you can instead gain control of a grappling confrontation by launching your own attack.

Self-defense is best accomplished by keeping your movements simple. If you find yourself lying on your back on the ground, your first course of action is to remove your opponent from his superior

Are They More Effective Than Gracie Jujutsu?

by Dr. Scott Shaw

upper position. Do not waste time attempting to block his punches. The best you can hope to accomplish is to shield your face with your arms while he attacks. A more effective response is to immediately take defensive measures and free yourself from his hold.

Removing an opponent from on top of you is best accomplished by finding, and disabling, the portion of his body that is stabilizing him. This is generally one of his arms, which is often anchored on the ground so he can punch you with his free arm. Because the stabilizing arm is stationary, it makes an easy target; you don't want to attempt to grab an arm that is in motion.

Once you identify the opponent's stabilizing limb, you must dislodge it. One option is to deliver a knifehand strike to

107

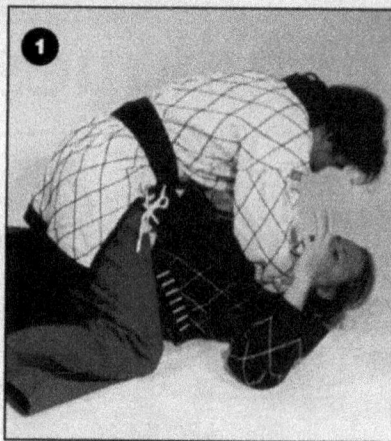

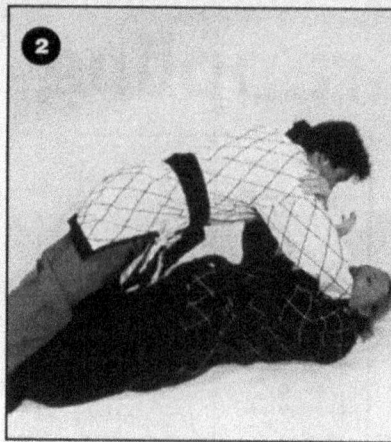

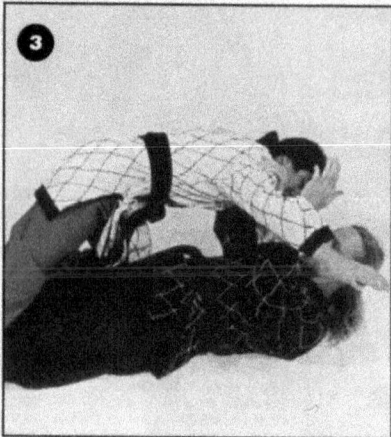

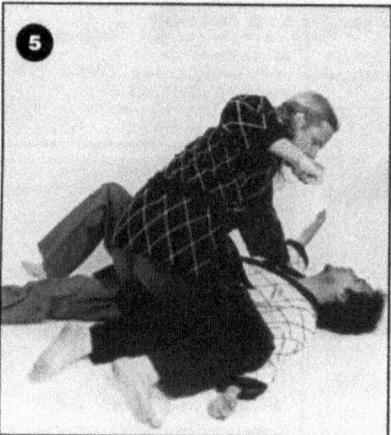

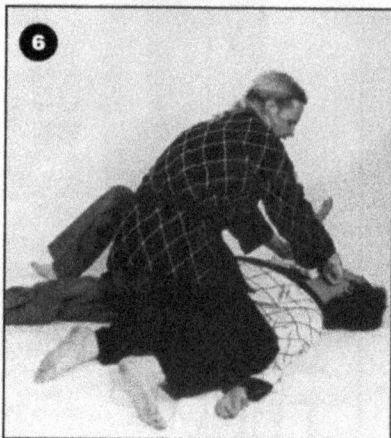

If an assailant has a hapkido stylist on his back and is choking him (1), the hapkido practitioner can deliver (2) a knifehand to the inside of the attacker's elbow joint, dislodging the arm. Using the attacker's shoulder as a pivot point, the defender can force (3) the assailant over onto his back (4), where the hapkido stylist can deliver (5-6) a punch to the jaw.

opponent's vital points and momentarily diverted his attention and/or loosened any hold he may have on you. If your opponent is on top of you, your choices are limited to a knuckle punch to his solar plexus, an eye gouge, or a palm strike to his nose. Once you have struck one of these locations, you can attempt to remove him from his upper position by reaching up with your other hand and grabbing the back of the opponent's head (or his hair), pulling it toward you as you apply pressure to his jaw. This two-handed technique will effectively lock his neck, allowing you to direct him off of you as you continue twisting his neck. Once you have removed him from his vantage point and you have assumed the upper position, you can deliver additional counterstrikes as necessary.

Obviously, it is best not to allow yourself to be placed on your back in the first place. You must therefore learn how to redirect an opponent's grappling attack so you emerge in the upper position.

You have three options when an opponent has initiated a frontal attack and forced you downward. First, you can deflect his attack while traveling toward the ground. If your opponent jumps at you, deflect one of his arms slightly to one side of your body as you are moving toward the ground. Although it may be too late to prevent a ground fight, the deflection maneuver allows you to land on the ground side by side with your opponent, instead of him being on top of you. Furthermore, if you keep your deflecting hand in place, near his shoulder, you can achieve a degree of control over him once you hit the ground. Control over the opponent is accomplished by maintaining pressure on the back of his shoulder, thus holding him facedown on the ground.

Once your opponent's initial attack has been nullified and you have assumed a level of control, you can deliver a punch to the back of his head or lock him in place with additional grappling techniques.

Your second course of action once you have been impacted and are traveling toward the ground is to grab hold of your opponent. The common response by most defenders is to grab the attacker's arm or clothing as they are falling. This serves little purpose, however You must be more scientific about where you grab the opponent as you are falling.

As mentioned, the opponent's neck is an ideal location to manipulate. The neck is easy to grab, and once you have taken hold of it, you can virtually control the opponent's entire body. Or, as you are

the inside of the opponent's elbow joint, collapsing his arm. By simultaneously taking hold of your opponent's shoulder, you can utilize it as a pivot point as you shove his arm behind his back, sending him over onto his back. Thus, you have gained the upper position.

If your opponent is using both arms to punch with and you cannot locate a sta-

bilizing base to attack, you will have to remove him from his upper position in a different manner To accomplish this, you must locate another part of his body to manipulate. The most likely choice is your opponent's neck.

In hapkido, it is understood that no joint manipulation should be attempted until you have first struck one of your

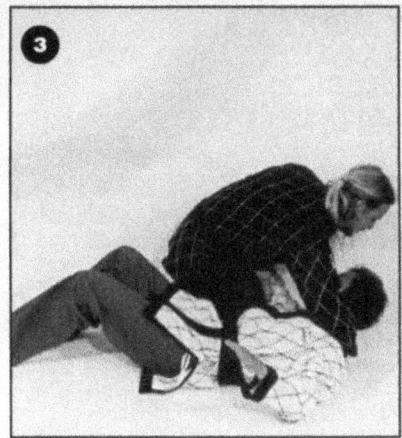

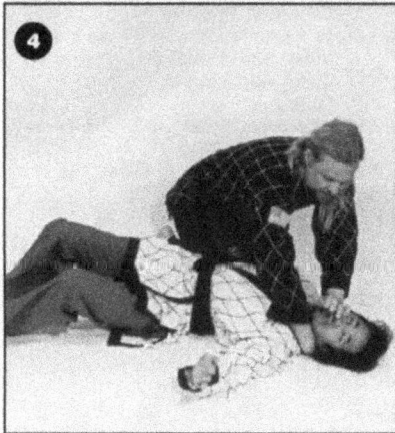

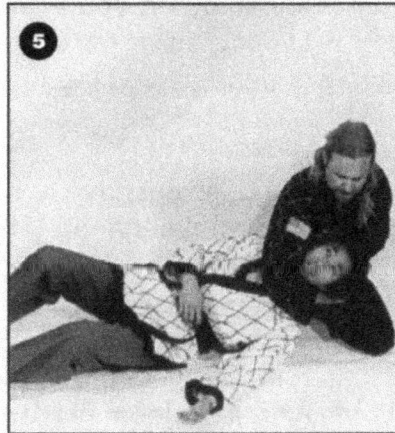

If an attacker lunges (1) at you, you can grab him (2) in a head lock as you both fall (3) to the ground. Once on the ground, you can immediately deliver (4) a palm heel to the jaw and place (5) the assailant in a painful head lock.

The final alternative, once your momentum is headed toward the ground, is to land on top of your opponent, placing you in a superior position. This maneuver can be accomplished by pivoting your

Continued on page 144

If an assailant is on top of you, attempting (1) to punch your face, you can respond by delivering (2) a palm heel to his nose. Grab the back of his neck and push (3) his jawbone, twisting as you direct him (4) off of you. Once you have superior position, you can deliver (5-6) a knifehand to his temple.

falling, you can put your opponent in a head lock. When you hit the ground, you can easily maintain control of him by

quickly sliding your arm around his neck until you have placed him in a painful choke hold.

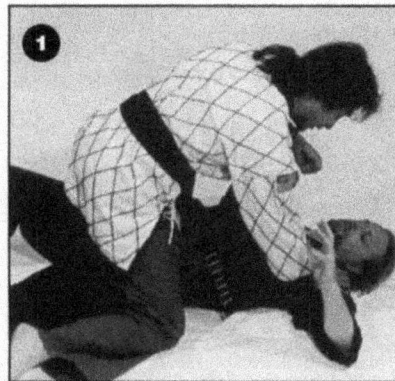

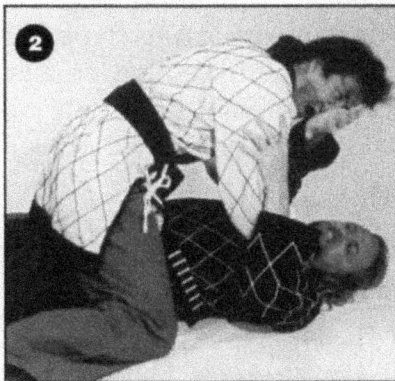

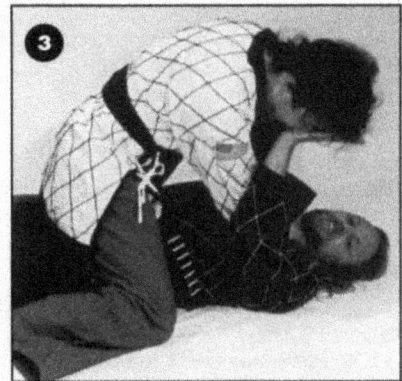

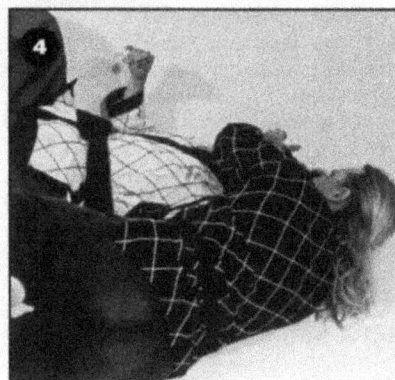

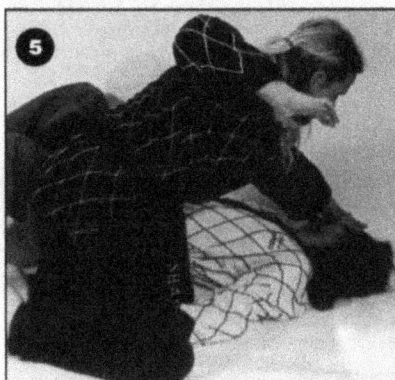

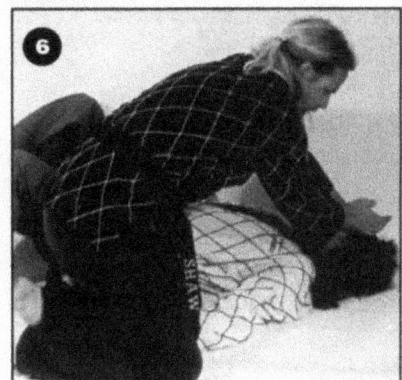

Hapkido Grappling Techniques

body as your opponent grabs you. By falling in this manner, you have the option of delivering an elbow strike to your opponent's head as you land.

***

Grappling does not have to be a complicated fighting experience. The key is to never allow your opponent to remain in a superior combat position. Instead, you should always take control of the encounter, make every move count, and leave nothing to random motion.

Practicing with a partner can give you a clearer understanding of the various elements of your opponent's body which will be exposed in each type of grappling situation. Such training enables you to learn how to effectively deal with an assailant in any type of grappling encounter ✖

About the author· Dr. Scott Shaw is a Hermosa Beach, California-based martial artist, actor and freelance writer.

Take 'Em Down!

Hapkido's Counters Against Korean Kicks

No practitioner of a traditional Korean martial art – Tae Kwon Do, Tang Soo Do, or Hapkido – would ever doubt the power and effectiveness of the Korean kicking arsenal. Due to the offensive prowess of Korean kicks, the debate has long gone on, however, of the most defensively effective way to deal with the onslaught of these very powerful kicking techniques. Here's how.

By Scott Shaw
Photos by Hae Won Shin

Each confrontational situation when an opponent launches a Korean kicking attack towards you, is of course dominated by its own set of circumstances. At times, a quick retreat from the attack of the kick, followed by a rapid counter-offensive advance may be called for. At other times, the only recourse may be to forcefully block the attack.

No matter what method is used to deal with the oncoming Korean kick, some type of defensive action must be taken or the power of the Korean kick will, no doubt, overpower even the most savvy of opponents.

It is the belief of the Hapkido practitioner that no defensive technique, be it a retreat from the oncoming kick or a block, should be performed solely as a means to

an end. Hapkido teaches the "Continual Motion Theory"; meaning, one technique must immediately follow the last. Toward

> It is the belief of the Hapkido practitioner that no defensive technique, be it a retreat from the oncoming kick or a block, should be performed solely as a means to an end. Hapkido teaches the "Continual Motion Theory"; meaning, one technique must immediately follow the last.

this end, the Hapkido practitioner will often first confront a kicking attack by defusing its power as close to its point of inception as possible. Then, immediately, follow through with a technique which will forcefully send the kicking opponent

to the ground. To understand Hapkido kick throws more completely, we must first view how an advancing kick is properly intercepted.

Intercepting a Kick

Your opponent has faced off with you. He has begun the process of throwing a roundhouse kick at you. Since the roundhouse kick is one of the most powerful of the Korean kicks — if you were to wait to block this offensive technique until the kick has been fully extended, you would no doubt be adversely effected by the power of the kick. This would be true even if you were to block the kick to some degree. Often the force of the roundhouse kick would send your blocking hands and arms smashing back into your face or body.

It is for this reason that you should counter any kick as close to its point of inception as possible. It is a far more effective kick blocking technique. In this way, the kick will not have developed a powerful velocity with the possibility of injuring you, even if you do effectively deliver a block against it.

Let's look at this roundhouse-kick blocking situation again. Your opponent is preparing to launch a roundhouse kick at you. This time, instead of waiting for it to come to you, you pivot off of your rear leg and move your forward leg slightly in, towards the oncoming roundhouse kick as you prepare to block it.

By traveling even this slight distance, you lessen the power or the kick, because it will not have the chance to fully develop. Furthermore, this very slight forward leg movement does not require much time or energy to complete. By preparing yourself to effectively block the kick, with just this slightest bit of movement, you will not be overpowered by the rapidly traveling roundhouse kick.

The moment you begin this forward motion into a more favorable position to block the oncoming kick, you must begin your roundhouse kick block as well. In Hapkido's Continuous Motion Theory we learn, "No movement, be it offensive or defensive, is of itself enough to emerge victorious from a confrontation."

Therefore, to move in and then begin to block not only slows your entire defensive technique down, but could ultimately lead to the offensive kick impacting on you. You must move into blocking pos-

Defense Against A Front Kick. From a starting position (1), your opponent kicks toward you and you step forward and encounter the kick's force with a cross-arm block (2). Grab hold of your opponent's kicking leg (3) and by lifting, throw him backwards to the ground (4).

To avoid being struck by the spinning heel kick, as your opponent launches it you can quickly step in toward his body. By doing this, you will now be inside of the kick's power. Once the back of his leg has made powerless contact to the biceps region of your forward arm, you can wrap your arm under his kicking leg. Now, by sweeping his base leg and pushing at his rear shoulder, he is easily sent to the ground.

ture immediately as you begin to move towards the kick.

Though there are several effective roundhouse kick blocking techniques, the leading mistake many martial artists make when encountering this kick is to attempt to block the kicking leg of their opponent with an open hand. The roundhouse kick is a very powerful weapon, due to the momentum it develops. Blocking it in open-hand fashion can easily lead to broken fingers.

One of the quickest, easiest and most effective methods of blocking the midsection-targeted roundhouse kick is to simply jam it. Allow the opponent's leg to make contact on your chest and his shin to contact you on the biceps region of your arm. The key to making this an effective block is to not allow the instep of your opponent's foot to make contact

with you. That's because the instep is the ideal impact tool of the roundhouse kick and it is where all of the kick's power is focused.

The most efficient way to not allow your opponent's instep to strike you is to close the gap between you and your opponent by stepping slightly in towards his body as he launches his roundhouse kick. This defense effortlessly works because you move both in towards the kick and close the distance between your opponent's body and your own. Thus, you will have effortlessly defused the majority of the power of this roundhouse kick.

After the Block

Once your opponent's roundhouse kick has been effortlessly blocked as discussed above, you should not assume that will be the end-all to the confrontation.

Defense Against An Ax Kick. From a starting position (1), your opponent attempts an ax kick (2). Before it can travel down, you step forward and encounter his leg with your shoulder (3). Grab his leg and send his back to the ground (4).

your opponent's heel making contact with its target. Therefore, with this kick, the heel is the object to avoid.

To avoid being struck by the spinning heel kick, as your opponent launches it, you can quickly step in toward his body. By doing this, you will now be inside of the kick's power. Once inside, as the kick travels towards you, take control of your opponent by allowing his leg to continue to travel to you, as we did with the roundhouse kick. Once the back of his leg has made powerless contact to the biceps region of your forward arm, you can wrap your arm under his kicking leg. Now, by sweeping his base leg and pushing at his rear shoulder, he is easily sent to the ground.

The Front Kick Counter

The Front kick, though one of the most basic offensive techniques in the Korean kicking arsenal, is no doubt one of the most penetrating and effective. To deal with it, you must first rapidly slide your body back as your opponent attempts to make front kick contact with you. By doing this, the front kick's target point will have moved and the power of the kick's muscle-driven force will keep it moving upward for a moment. As you move back, you should simultaneously perform a cross-arm block to the shin of your opponent.

The cross arm block is executed by crossing your arms at just below elbow level, and allowing the front kick to impact where your two arms meet. Thus, your opponent's front kick will impact

For if you end your self-defense with a block, your opponent will, no doubt, launch further attacks at you.

Again, in Hapkido's Continuous Motion Theory it is taught, "We must always continue forward with additional techniques until our opponent is defeated." In the case of the roundhouse-kick block, you must move on with additional defensive techniques to assure your victory.

You have now blocked the roundhouse kick, instead of allowing your opponent to quickly pull his leg back to regain his footing, you must immediately take control of the confrontation and grab hold of it. You can most effectively achieve this by continuing through with your blocking arm motion and wrapping your arm around his leg.

Now that you have substantial con-

trol over him, you can rapidly step through, behind his leg. And now, by simply shoving him back at his shoulder level with your free hand as you simultaneously sweep-kick him, he will be thrown to the ground.

We now understand that our Korean kick-blocking techniques must remain simple, and thus very fast, which will cause them to be quite effective.

The Spinning Heel Kick Counter

The spinning heel kick is very similar in form and structure to the roundhouse kick. It is a circular, momentum-driven kick. Thus, it is dealt with in a similar fashion to that of the roundhouse kick.

The spinning heel kick is one of the most powerful kicks in the Korean kicking arsenal. Its impact power comes from

One of the quickest, easiest and most effective methods of blocking the midsection-targeted roundhouse kick is to simply jam it. Allow the opponent's leg to make contact on your chest and his shin to contact you on the biceps region of your arm. The key to making this an effective block is to not allow the instep of your opponent's foot to make contact with you. That's because the instep is the ideal impact tool of the roundhouse kick and it is where all of the kick's power is focused.

Defense Against A Roundhouse Kick. From a starting position (1), your opponent attempts a roundhouse kick at you. Step in toward his body, thus missing the forceful impact of the kick (2). You allow the diffused kick to make contact with your body. Catch your opponent's kicking leg and take control of it (3). With the aid of a shove and a sweep, (4) send him to the ground (5).

into strong bone and muscle mass, which will leave you free from injury.

Once you have stepped back and blocked the oncoming front kick, you must immediately wrap your hands down and around your opponent's kicking leg before he has the ability to get his kicking foot back on the ground. Once you have made this grab, you must instantly lift your opponent's leg up, while forcing his knee back into his body. This will send him flying backwards to the ground.

The muscles of the leg are much stronger than that of the arms. Thus, you are actually at a grasping disadvantage when you hold an opponent's leg in this fashion. Therefore, this Hapkido throwing technique must be executed very rapidly for it to become a useful defensive application.

The Side Kick Counter

The traditional Korean side kick, due

You should counter any kick as close to its point of inception as possible. It is a far more effective kick blocking technique. In this way, the kick will not have developed a powerful velocity with the possibility of injuring you, even if you do effectively deliver a block against it.

to its very linear nature, is effectively dealt with in a similar cross-arm-block fashion, as with the front kick. The first line of defense is to slide your body back slightly, as your opponent launches his kick, thus nullifying the side kick's power.

Then, once you are out of harm's way, you must immediately take control of the kicking advance with a cross-arm block and lock technique, (as we performed with the front kick). Now that you have gained control over your opponent's offensive technique, simply by pulling back on his leg, he will lose his balance and fall to the floor.

The Ax Kick Counter

It is the upward linear thrusting motion of the front kick which gives it its force and power. In the reverse, it is the forceful downward motion of the ax kick which allows it to be a devastating tool of offensive destruction.

The ax kick is first forcefully brought

1

2

3

4

5

Defense Against A Spinning Heel Kick. From a starting position (1), your opponent begins a spinning heel kick. You step in towards your opponent, inside the kick's power (2). You allow his kicking leg to continue through, as you take control of it (3). You allow his motion to continue its spin, as you pivot on your base leg (4). With the aid of a leg lift, a sweep, and a push to the shoulder, your opponent is sent to the ground (5).

up and then powerfully down onto the shoulder of an opponent. With this impact, the collar bone is easily broken. The general method for dealing with the ax kick is to step out of its path. Though this is no doubt one of the best methods of defense against the ax kick, at times you may need to be more assertive in your handling of an aggressive opponent who has launched one of them. When this is the case, do just the opposite — jam the kick.

Your opponent launches an ax kick at you. As it raises up, you first lean out of its range. Then, before it has the opportunity to travel downward, you must rapidly move into its path.

The impact point of the ax kick is the heel of your opponent's foot. Again, as with the other kicks we have discussed, you must avoid being struck by any kick's actual focus of power.

By rapidly moving in toward your opponent, you impact your shoulder into

Though there are several effective roundhouse kick blocking techniques, the leading mistake many martial artists make when encountering this kick is to attempt to block the kicking leg of their opponent with an open hand. The roundhouse kick is a very powerful weapon, due to the momentum it develops. Blocking it in open-hand fashion can easily lead to broken fingers.

the calf of his leg, below his heel. From here, you must quickly reach around his kicking leg, taking control of it. As his kicking leg has now been trapped against your shoulder, you forcefully move closer towards him. With this forward motion, his kicking leg is forced against himself. Then, by releasing your grasp, as you continue to push his leg back, he is easily thrown backwards, onto the ground.

As you have now come to learn, simply blocking a kick is never your ultimate method of defense once you are under attack by a kicking adversary. Instead, it is to your confrontational advantage to take control of your opponent's kicking leg and send him forcefully to the ground, where his additional offensive actions will be seriously hindered. ∎

Scott Shaw is a Hermosa Beach, California-based actor, black belt and freelance writer.

Hapkido Knife Defense

Don't Get Stuck

By Scott Shaw

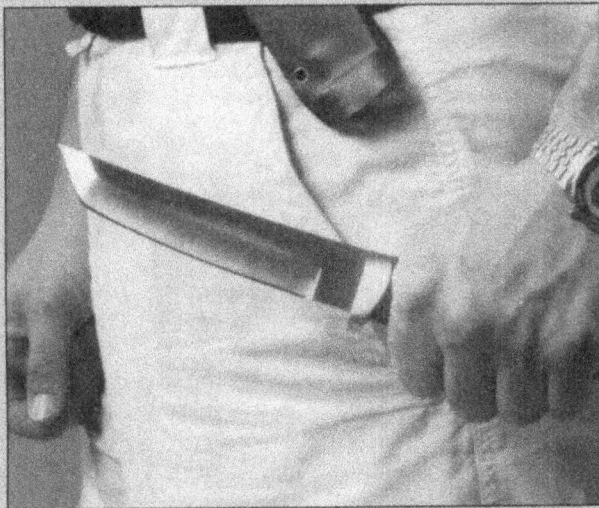

As random acts of violence have continued to grasp all aspects of modern society, we as competent martial artists must continually refine our methods of self defense in order to successfully protect ourselves and those we love if the need ever arises. The knife has long been one of the leading weapons of aggressive offensive behavior It is for this reason, we must place the knife at the forefront of our study of overall self defense, so we will not fall victim to its potentially deadly attack.

Whenever an opponent comes at you with a knife, you must immediately assume they mean you no good. With this understanding in mind, you must instantaneously launch into the most effective and powerful self defense possible to save yourself from potential injury.

To begin the study of self defense against the knife, you must first fully understand that unlike other weapons, such as a club, a knife has the potential to injure you, from any position, until your opponent has been completely disabled. For example, if you simply try to recklessly grab a hold and wrestle with your opponent's knife wielding hand, he can easily shift the direction of the knife and cut you. For this reason, it is of paramount importance, in knife self defense, you must first learn how to effectively intercept your opponent's knife holding arm and then immediately take control of his movements so he will not have the potential to injure you.

Interception of an opponent's knife holding hand is the first step which will lead to your overall control of the altercation. This is, however the most difficult thing to successfully accomplish, because of the fact your opponent will generally keep his knife holding hand in motion as he is attacking you.

The interception of the knife holding hand must take place as close to the inception of the altercation as possible. For with each

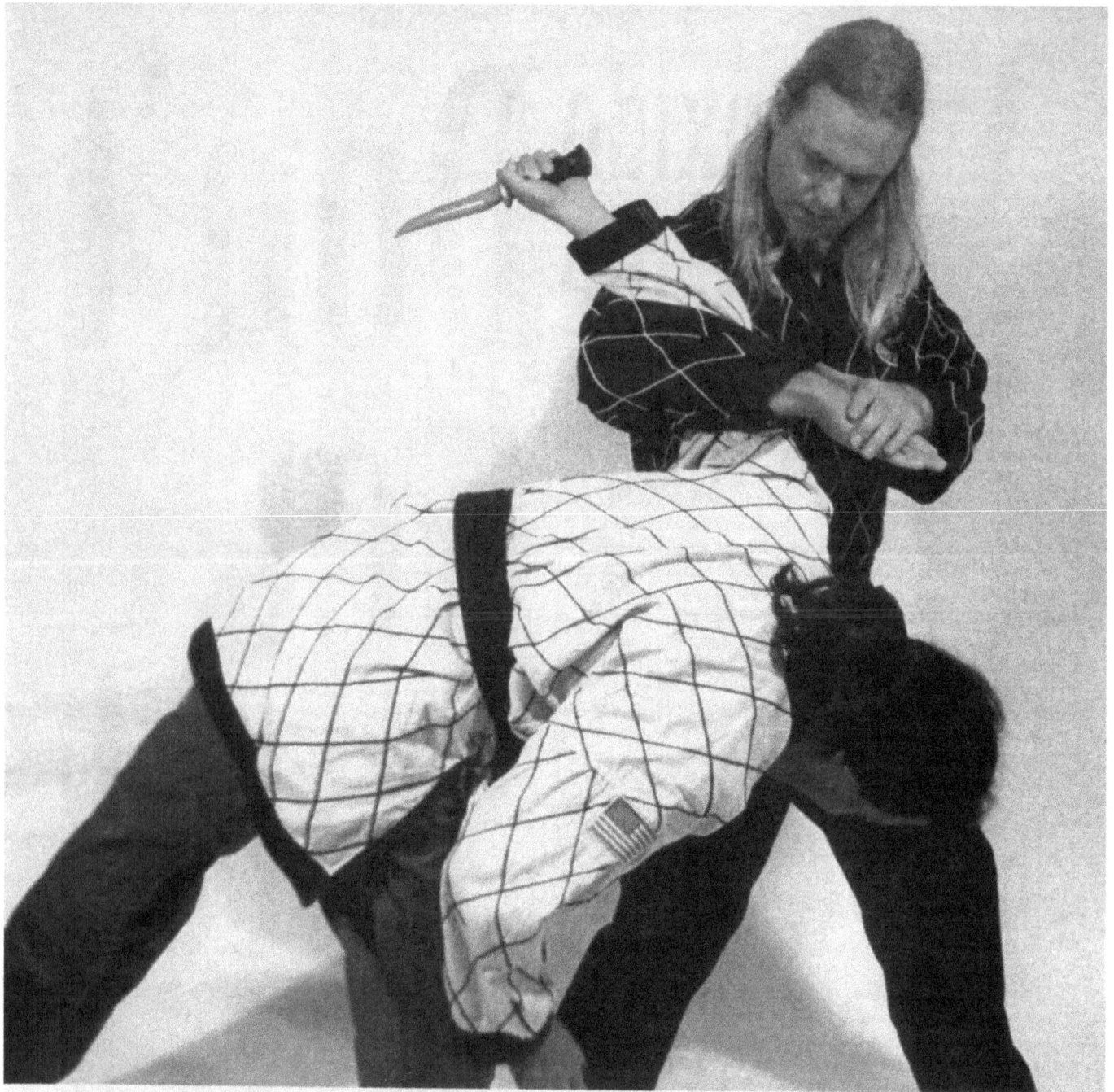

Your attacker is holding a knife on you (1). Immediately step in to him, deflecting his arm outwards (2). Bring your deflecting hand under and then over his arm (3). By impacting it across his elbow you lock his arm (4).

passing moment, your opponent has the ability to injure you with his knife.

There are two pathways to intercepting the arm of a knife wielding opponent. One, is to rapidly move in and encounter the arm before it has the opportunity to stab in your direction. The second, is for you to encounter your opponent's stabbing motion, as the knife is traveling towards you, and take control of it. Though, if performed improperly, either one of these knife intercepting pathways could prove dangerous. The second is potentially much more hazardous, however as the knife is in motion. To this end, it is to your advantage to move in and take control over your opponent's knife holding arm before he ever begins a stabbing technique.

The moment you are accosted by a knife holding attacker is when you must take immediate action. For example, if your opponent has just located himself in front of you and is standing with a knife pointing in your direction, threatening you, this is your ideal opportunity to move in towards him and take control of the altercation. You must do this before the attack escalates and the advantage substantially moves to your attacker

To effectively achieve knife defense with a stationary opponent, you must not try to grab randomly in the direction of his hand holding the blade. This is because, if he sees your oncoming motion and slightly shifts the knife, you hand could be easily cut. It is a far better initial form of knife defense, if you take control of him by other more refined, means.

The best and simplest way to effectively encounter a stationary "knife holding" opponent is to rapidly move in towards him, allowing your lead leg to slide you forward. As you precisely move in towards him, you move slightly to his outside, angling your body out of the direct pathway of the knife. Simultaneously as you move in, you extend your lead arm with an Open Palm. With this Open Palm leading, you impact to the outside forearm of your opponent's knife holding arm. Once you have made contact, you powerfully shove his forearm tightly against this body. This will give you initial control over his motions.

As this lead-in technique will only control your adversary momentarily, you must immediately deliver a devastating blow to keep him from regaining his footing and launching a secondary knife attack at you. The type of strikes which would be most appropriate, are a Straight Punch to his temple or a Knife Hand to his throat with your free hand.

Another effective method to encounter a stationary 'knife wielding' opponent is to rapidly move in and joint lock his knife holding arm. This can be successfully accomplished by, again, allowing your forward leg to rapidly guide you in towards your opponent. As you do so, you have your forward arm move in and deflect his knife holding arm outwards. This is achieved by making your lead-in hand into a knife hand. You move in and strike to your opponent's inner forearm region, with a forty-five degree, downward, knife hand technique. This will effectively drive his knife holding arm outwards and away from you.

Once this initial deflection is made, you must immediately continue forward with additional controlling maneuvers. Because now that you have begun your defense, your opponent will no doubt be much more agitated and will attempt to cut you.

To utilize the least amount of energy in this knife defense technique, you should follow through with your initial deflecting path and allow your lead-in arm to slide rapidly downward, along the knife holding arm of your opponent. This will check his arm and keep him from stabbing at you as you continue forward with your technique. As you step in closer to him, you immediately send your deflecting arm under and then over the top of his arm. This forces his knife holding arm to extend out straight. You continue forward with this technique and you locate your

Photos by Hae Won Shin

Your opponent attempts to make a low level stab at you (1). Stop its path with a Cross Wrist Block (2). Immediately take a hold of his knife holding hand, with your thumb to the central back region of it and your fingers wrapped around his palm (3). Arch it against itself, locking it (4). Further control his arm, by placing a powerful Palm Hand to his elbow (5).

121

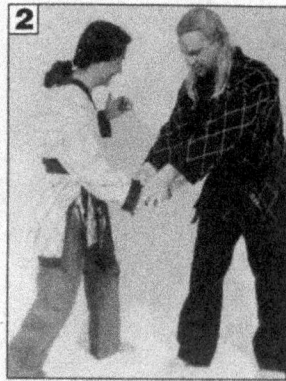

Your attacker makes a low level stab at you (1). Encounter his stab with double Circle Hand blocks (2). Immediately pivot your body, while directing his arm, up and over your head (3). Then, drive the knife into his own midsection (4-5).

arm to the rear elbow region of your opponent. By powerfully forcing downward on this hold, to his elbow, you lock his entire arm. Thus, he will not be able to launch a secondary attack at you.

Though taking control over an knife possessing opponent before he ever moves his blade forward to attack you is the ideal circumstance, it is not always possible. For this reason, you must learn to successfully defend against a knife attack, once the blade is in motion.

There are a few consistent paths a knife attacker will generally take when attempting to stab. We can isolate these movements and, thereby, learn how best to deal with them.

One of the key things to watch for whenever an attacker has accosted you with a knife is shoulder movement. Your opponent will generally move the shoulder on the side which possesses the knife, just a bit, before he actually sends the knife forward. This shoulder movement take place either because your opponent uses this motion to recoil his knife backwards just a small amount before he launches it forward with additional momentum or he will slightly move his shoulder to realign himself, to better frame the path of his knife attack. In either case, movement in your opponent's shoulder is the clue to watch for when a knife attack is at hand. Once you observe this shoulder motion, this is your time to prepare for the oncoming blade.

When an opponent stabs towards your midsection with a low level knife attack, it is imperative you keep the knife as far away from your body as possible. To achieve this, you must meet the forward thrusting attack of the knife as close to its point of inception as possible. To do this you can effectively encounter your opponent's knife trusting arm with a Cross Wrist Block as you additionally arch your back outwards, at your lower spine level. This arching will give you added distance between your stomach and the blade.

The Cross Wrist Block is accomplished by crossing your two hands, in knife hand fashion, at your wrists, forming a firm arch. You send your knife blocking arms forward and downward at a forty-five degree angle, impacting your opponent to his knife thrusting forearm. This will halt the onslaught of the blade.

Once this attack is blocked, you must immediately proceed through with additional measures to keep your opponent from refocusing and launching a secondary attack. Therefore, you instantly allow your block to slide back near your opponent's knife holding hand. From here, you reach in with your rear hand, (the one closest to his knife holding hand), and place your thumb to the central back portion of his hand. As you do this, your fingers powerfully wrap around his knife holding palm. Immediately, you arch his wrist unnaturally to the side and ninety degrees backwards, against itself. Thus, locking it.

Now that you have taken control of his wrist, you can easily guide his arm by putting additional pressure to this wrist lock.

You extend his arm out straight. Then, you combine the wrist lock with a powerful shove to the back of his elbow. His wrist, elbow, and thus his body are completely locked. He can not continue on with his attack.

Knife attacks are also commonly directed at your mid section or your head, by your opponent making sideways stabbing or slashing motions. The key to encountering this type of knife attack is to, again, meet your opponent's oncoming arm motion as close to its point of inception as possible. By blocking the knife's path as soon as possible, a sufficient amount of momentum will not have been developed by your opponent's arm to keep the knife traveling through your block and, thus, making impact to your body.

Your opponent launches a head level, circular slashing knife assault. You instantaneously stops the knife's progress by per-

122

Your opponent attempts an overhead stab (1). Block its progress with a Cross Body High Block (2). Place the middle finger of your free hand into his elbow joint (3). Shove his knife holding arm back onto itself, locking it (4).

forming a knife hand, In-to-Out Cross Arm Block to your opponent's inner forearm region. This will keep your blocking arm a sufficient distance away form the knife so it can not easily shift and cut you.

Once you have blocked the initial knife attack, immediately bring your free arm up and under impacting it to the backside of your opponent's attacking arm, just below his elbow. This will give you controlling leverage. With the arm you initially blocked with, you shove your opponent's forearm back against itself. This will keep your opponent from having the ability to redirect the knife. With your bracing arm, take a hold of your opponent's knife holding wrist from behind as you bend his arm back farther, unnaturally behind itself. You have now locked your opponent. He will not have the ability to launch a secondary knife attack.

Overhead, downward stabbing, knife assaults are also a common type of attack. Again, as in all forward moving knife assaults, you must block it as close to its point of inception as possible.

Your opponent attempts to stab you with an overhead attack. By immediately performing a Cross Body High Block to your opponent's knife wielding forearm, you stop the motion of his oncoming knife. Once you have initially blocked it, you immediately place the middle finger of your free hand into his knife holding elbow joint. By reaching your thumb around the bottom of his elbow, you take a powerful hold. This grabbing technique gives you powerful leverage. As you perform this grab, you simultaneously shove his arm back against itself, powerfully locking it. From this positioning you can effortlessly control your opponent.

As each type of knife attack is different, the specific type of defense you use must be designed to effectively deal with the path of the oncoming blade. Therefore, it is very important to study and practice the various methods of knife defense to keep yourself free from injury and victorious in the confrontation, if your are ever attacked by a knife wielding opponent.

123

Hapkido
Vs.
Street
Weapons

With the growing proliferation of violent crime in our streets, the use of weapons is often directly linked to these crimes. We as martial artists must learn an effective way to defend and take control of a situation where an assailant, who, possessing a weapon, has accosted us with less than sociable behavior in mind.

By Scott Shaw

Photos by Joel Ciniero

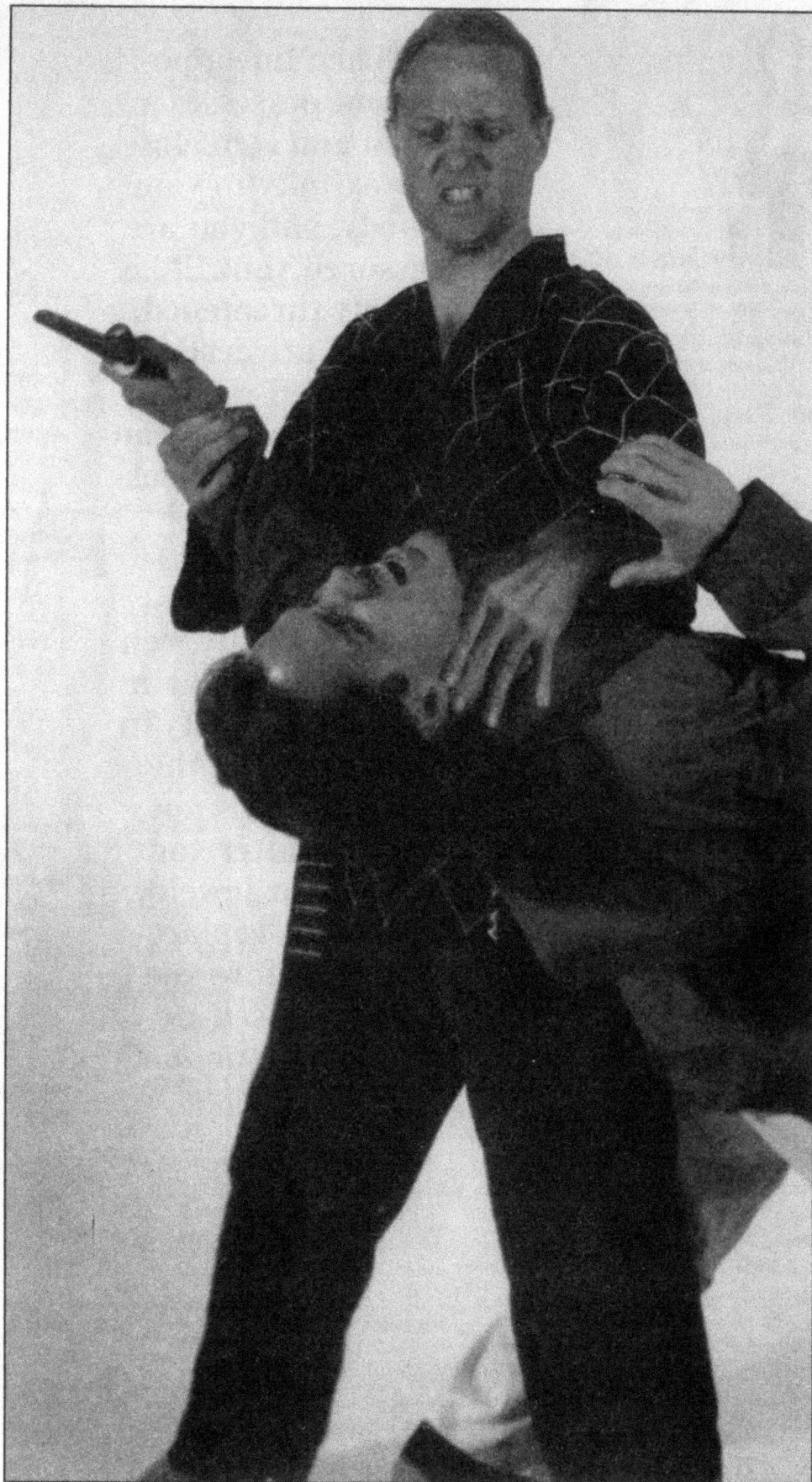

The key element in the initial mastery of weapon self-defense is to discard any technique that is too elaborate to be truly effective in the street. Often, in martial art demonstrations and as taught in the dojo alike, techniques are demonstrated that, though visually beautiful, have little effectiveness when placed in competition against that of a trained streetfighting opponent.

With this fact in mind, we can begin our view of what type of technique is most effective against the use of the various types of weapons most commonly found in a streetfight, and the most appropriate way of dealing with them.

Run from a Gun

The issue of guns is often the first question brought up in street self-defense. Guns are no doubt the most dangerous of all weapons now commonly found on the street. If your opponent possesses a gun and is at any distance from you, the best thing you can do is run. The speed a bullet travels, and the likelihood of it having the ability to fatally injure you, are too great a risk to ever take a chance against. Especially if your opponent is truly willing to use his gun and is more than a few feet away from you.

When the opponent possesses a gun and is in close proximity to your body, and you are assured your life is truly threatened, there are certain basic self-defense techniques that can be used to deflect it. Again, the squeezing of a trigger is so fast and so deadly, you must be sure your life is ultimately in danger and the assailant is not simply after your money or jewelry, which is replaceable, before you put any self-defense into action.

The quickest and, no doubt, the simplest way to defend against a gun, from a frontal attack, in very close proximity to your body, is to simply rapidly deflect it with an in-to-out forearm block and then quickly

> When the opponent possesses a gun and is in close proximity to your body, and you are assured your life is truly threatened, there are certain basic self-defense techniques that can be used to deflect it. Again, the squeezing of a trigger is so fast and so deadly, you must be sure your life is ultimately in danger and the assailant is not simply after your money or jewelry, which is replaceable, before you put any self-defense into action.

strike the opponent with a devastating blow. This means, a knife hand to his throat, or, perhaps, a palm strike under his nose. By defending against the gun in this fashion, even if the trigger is pulled, with any luck your deflection will be rapid enough to have the bullet fly off, hurting no one.

This type of simplistic gun defense and immediate follow through with a powerful counterstrike is effective if the assailant is close in front of you, or if he holds a gun

directly to your back, from the rear. In each case, you know the exact location of the weapon, and, thus, this defense can be effective.

Improper Knife Strategies

More common, as they have much more availability, is the use of knife and clubs in street altercations. The defense against these weapons, though potentially equally as deadly as a hand gun, is much more controllable with the calculable results being much more promising.

The knife, as a common weapon on the street, has long been documented. Every martial art style has consciously devised its own individual methods to deal with the knife's oncoming blade. There is, however, one universal truth that comes into play when defending against the knife; that is, to never meet its assault by attempting to grab the blade or the hand of the assailant holding the knife.

If you should encounter a knife attack head on, what then is the most appropriate method to deal with it once an assailant has wielded one at you? The key element is deflection. No matter what form of counterattack you choose to launch once the oncoming blade has been moved from a direct line between you and your body, it must be deflected first before any further maneuvering can successfully be accomplished.

Many martial art styles have devised methods for you to move in rapidly and catch the arm of your opponent who possesses a knife before he launches an attack at you. Catching, however, is not very effective for three reasons. First, because the arm of the opponent generally moves too fast for you to be sure that in any instant you will have the ability to reach in and catch it with the hope of then performing some elaborate technique and ultimately disarming him from his knife.

Your opponent attempts a low-level knife stab at you (1). You slightly step back, out of the knife's range, and deflect your opponent's knife-bearing arm (2). By continuing through with the deflection and taking control of your assailant's arm (3), you direct his arm and the knife to your opponent's chest area (4), where his arm and the knife are locked. He can now be thrown to the ground or you may now take further offensive measures.

There is one universal truth that comes into play when defending against the knife; that is, to never meet its assault by attempting to grab the blade or the hand of the assailant holding the knife.

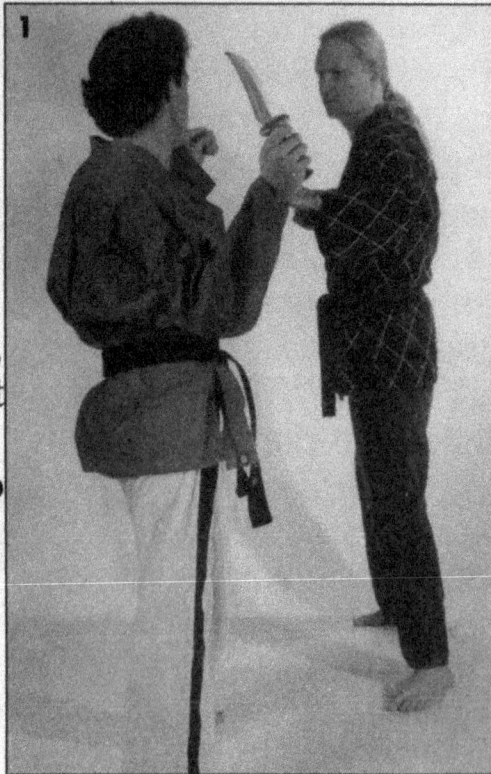

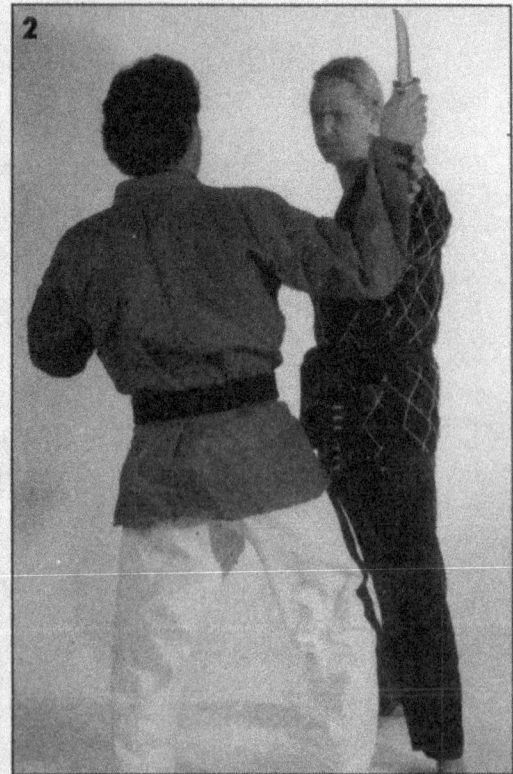

Deflection is the key element to successfully defend against a knife. Deflection occurs at the moment your opponent begins to extend his arm. For at this point he is the most vulnerable to deflection.

Your opponent attempts a high-level knife slash at you (1). You intercept his movement by catching his arm, as it is incoming, with the section of your hand between your thumb and first finger (2). From here, you instantly lock his wrist (3) and perform a strike to your opponent's throat (4).

128

Second, be aware that the avid streetfighter has the ability to see your hands moving towards him in order to catch his arm holding the knife. If you do attempt to grab his arm, all he has to do is slightly move and you will have left yourself prone to an easy attack by his knife.

The third problem with attempting to catch your opponent's knife-holding arm is that, when and if you can accomplish this, he will not remain in one position allowing you to control him and perform whatever type of self-defense technique you have planned. No, he will not. Inevitability, he will simply shift the knife in his hand slightly and cut you. Though this cut may inflict less damage than the straight-ahead assault of his knife to your body. Nonetheless, getting cut is to no one's advantage.

As dangerous as it is to try to rush in on a knife-wielding opponent, it is also not a good idea to rapidly move towards your armed opponent with the hope of defeating him with a punch or kick. He possesses the knife and any movement that you may make, as stylized as it may be, allows him the ability to stab you with the knife to whatever part of your body with which you attempt to attack him.

Proper Knife Strategy

Now that we understand what not to do, though these erroneous techniques are taught in many martial art schools, how then do we effectively defend against the knife? As mentioned, deflection is the key element to successfully defend against this very deadly weapon.

The assailant who possesses a knife inevitably will attempt to stab you with it. Whether or not he moves it around in an effort to confuse you as to its actual impact point is irrelevant, for sooner or later its blade will be launched in at you. Deflection occurs at the moment your opponent begins to extend his arm. For at this point he is the most vulnerable to deflection. This is due to the fact that his arm being extended is in a more linear mode than when it is held in tight to his body, with his elbow bent. The bent elbow gives the opponent's arm much more power to forcefully resist any type of deflection you may perform.

So, for these reasons, it is better to wait for the arm of your opponent to be somewhat extended before you take action against his knife attack.

Knife deflection can be most effectively accomplished by waiting for your opponent to make the move to stab at you, as

There are two methods of dealing with the club-type weapon: one is to deflect its onslaught as described with that of the knife. The second is to directly block its oncoming strike and then follow through with the appropriate technique to end your assailant's further advances.

discussed, and then deflecting it in the most natural pattern your hand and arm may take. There are two types of knife deflections that are very effective from a low-level stabbing assault.

One is to deflect your opponent's arm, which holds his knife, in a downward in-to-out forearm block. By deflecting it, the knife has not been allowed to penetrate your zone of safety and you can immediately follow through with a counterstriking technique.

The second effective knife deflection technique, at low level, is to slightly step back, once the knife is launched, allowing the slashing knife to pass you by. You then must immediately take control of your opponent's arm which holds the knife, by checking it into place, perhaps by letting him continue through with the force of his own momentum, and then letting your arm take control of his knife-holding arm and locking it tight to his body. This way, he will not be able to stab at you a second time, while you immediately counterstrike.

In all knife-deflection techniques it is important that you never grab your opponent's hand or arm in such a manner that it will allow your opponent to come back and easily cut you. This is generally accomplished by never locking yourself into a deflection technique so tightly you cannot quickly and effectively move out of it and onto another one. For by remaining stiffly molded into any knife-defense

technique, it allows your opponent the added ability to shift his knife at wrist level and cut you.

Knife assaults that come at you from higher levels are deflected in similar patterns and methods as the lower ones previously described. The difference at this level, when the adversary slashes at approximate shoulder level, is that these leave your opponent opened to much stronger counterattacks once his knife has been deflected. Useful counterstrikes at this level, once the knife is deflected and checked into place, are front kicks to the opponent's knee or groin, or palm strikes under his nose.

As no one can give you exact specifications of what to do or what not to do, since each knife attack situation is defined by its own constraints, you must use judgment of which defense is best in any given knife-assault situation. The key elements to remember are:

1) That knife deflection is always preferable to direct encounters with a knife.

2) Once a knife has been deflected the opponent's knife-wielding arm must be checked so it cannot immediately launch a secondary attack on you.

3) Any deflection and arm check must be rapidly followed by a strong and debili-

Your opponent attempts a club swing at you (1). You step back, allowing it to miss and the momentum to carry him through (2 & 3). Instantly you hook kick him (4).

tating counterattack to prohibit your assailant from launching further assaults on you.

Clubs, Chains, Etc.

The third weapon often used on the street is that of a pipe, chain, club, or other similar elongated striking object that is used to hit your body. This type of weapon is perhaps the most commonly used weapon on the street since various versions of it are often readily at hand. One may find a large stick, or loose piece of pipe, anywhere. Though these weapons differ slightly in their make up, to defend against them one uses similar techniques. To this end we must study effective defenses against their attack.

There are two methods of dealing with the club-type weapon: one is to deflect its onslaught as described with that of the knife. The second is to directly block its oncoming strike and then follow through with the appropriate technique to end your assailant's further advances.

Deflection of this type of weapon is as

equally effective as it is with the knife blade. In the case of the club or the chain, it is even more effective than that of the knife, since the motion of this type of weapon cannot easily be altered and its make up does not allow its user to simply shift its impact point and cut you.

As these weapons are generally swung, simple deflection is accomplished by simply stepping out of the way of whatever impact point your attacker is attempting to find on your body, and then powerfully counterattacking. No doubt one of the most effective deflection techniques against the club or chain is, once it is launched in a side-to-side assault, is to simply step back and allow the force created by the weapon's swing to carry the arm of your opponent through. Then, instantly, you counterstrike with a powerful kick, such as the stepping side kick, to the opponent's body or with a hook kick to his head.

Deflection of these types of weapons can be aided by the use of checking your opponent's arm in one place once his initial assault has missed. This is not always necessary, however, as the club, chain, pipe, or similar weapon are clumsy weapons by their very design. An arm check may slow your counterstrike down and thus give your opponent the ability to launch a secondary attack at you with another hand or foot technique. Therefore, when encountering this type of weapon, it is perhaps best to simply move from its strike and rapidly and powerfully counterstrike before your opponent has the ability to realign his energies.

At times it is necessary to directly block the strike of a club. This is, in fact, generally quite easily accomplished, simply by intercepting your opponent in mid-strike positioning. The most appropriate time to block his club strike is, of course, as close to its beginning point as possible. By impacting it here, not only has his striking arm, which holds the weapon, not had the time to develop much velocity, but as well your arm will not be easily injured in the block, due to the fact that your opponent's striking arm has not developed full swing power.

The blocks against the pipe and other club type weapons should be focused at your opponent's mid-forearm. At this focus point not only is your opponent most susceptible to an effective block, but blocking your forearm to your opponent's forearm allows you to have a certain amount of range of extra movement and compensation if your assailant moves his technique

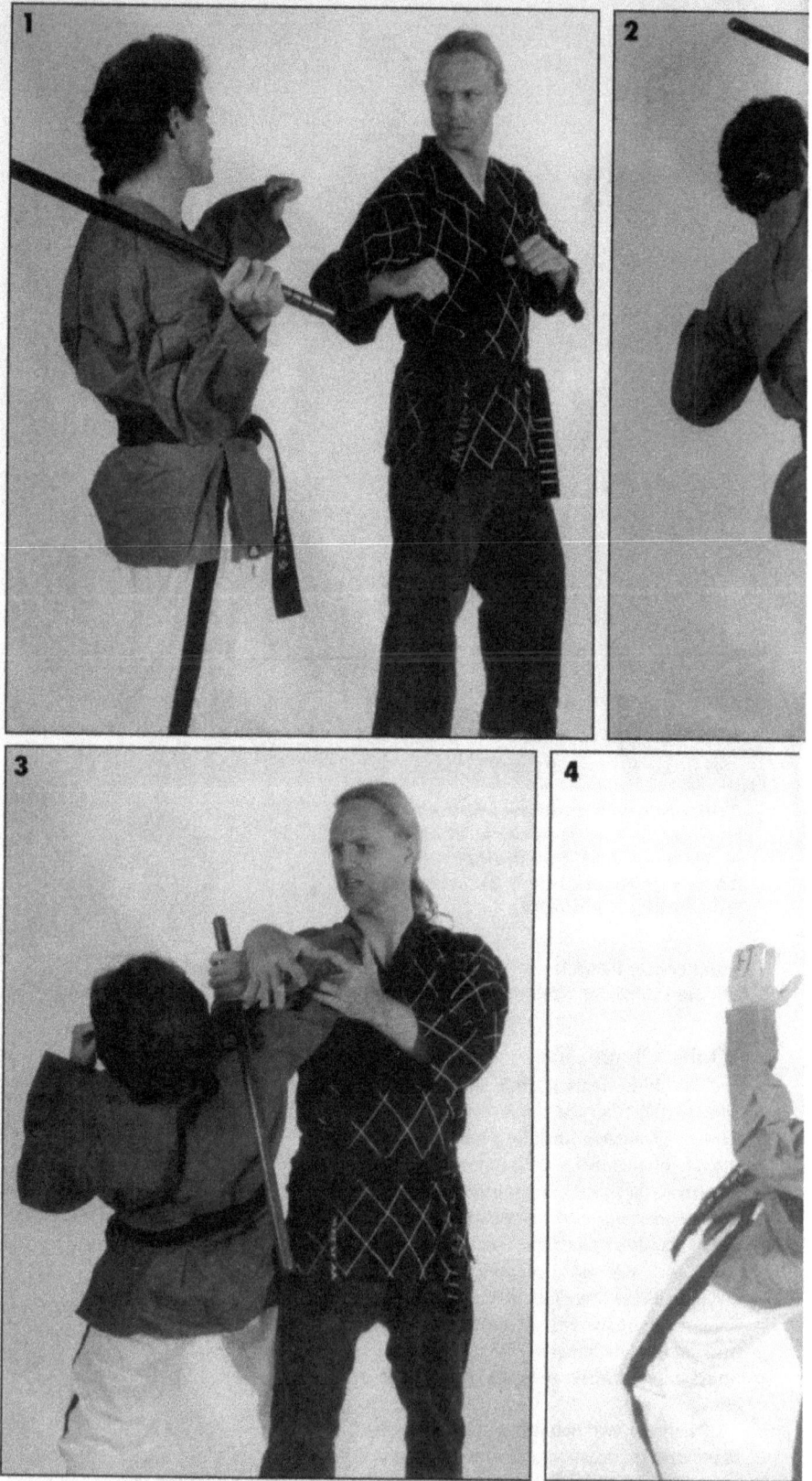

Your opponent attempts an overhead strike with a club (1). You block the attack in its early stages (2) and lock his arm by placing the middle finger of your free hand in his elbow joint (3). You simultaneously powerfully shove back his arm as you pivot, throwing him to the ground (4).

132

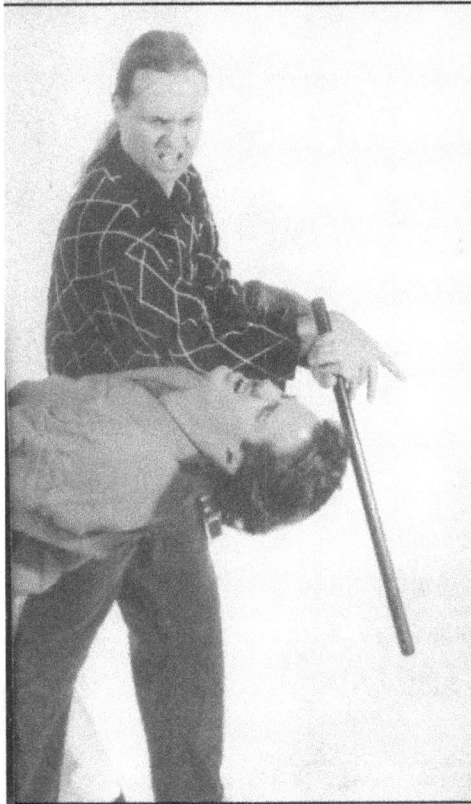

slightly

To attempt to simply catch your opponent's strike with your hand is generally a mistake. First of all, your hand, in size and range, is much smaller than your forearm. If you miss that initial catch, you will be struck by the club. Second, if you do, in fact, catch the attack of the oncoming club, what do you do then?

Catching and then holding your opponent's arm or wrist gives him several advantages in the confrontation, since he can effectively strike you with his other hand, or kick you with his knees or legs, while you struggle with his weapon-bearing arm and attempt to keep him from hitting you with the club.

By blocking the pipe attack with your forearm, you can easily shift into appropriate locking, throwing or counterstriking techniques with other parts of your body. For example, once you have halted the advance of the club towards you by blocking it, forearm to forearm, you can then easily and effectively lock your opponent's striking arm by rapidly placing the middle finger of your other hand into his elbow joint, using it as a bending point, and then powerfully shoving your opponent's arm back over itself. From this positioning you can easily lock him into submission, strike him, or forcefully throw him to the ground.

Partner Practice

There can be no hard and fast rule as to what defensive technique to use against the attempted strike of a club, pipe, stick or chain, (just as with the knife). The only way any martial artist can develop the appropriate eye-to-hand coordination necessary to be effective in the defense against any weapon is to practice with partners in a controlled environment in order to understand what techniques are truly effective in any given confrontational situation. The key element to make this type of partner practice effective is to not allow any block to work, unless it truly blocks your attack, to not allow any joint lock to lock you, unless it truly does, and to not allow any throw to throw you, unless it really does.

Fighting against weapons in a street confrontation is no one's idea of fun. It is, however, necessary that we learn effective defense against them just in case we ever encounter them on the street.

Scott Shaw is a professional writer and filmmaker who lives in Hermosa Beach, California.

133

The Hapkido
CANE
Street Legal Weaponry

The Korean art of Hapkido offers an extensive array of specialized cane techniques. The cane, being one of the last items of fashion which can also double as a weapon, can provide the user with a hidden and instant form of effective self-defense.

By Scott Shaw, PhD.

The humble walking stick is viewed by many as simply a tool that may aid the aged or those who have difficulty in walking. The Korean martial art of Hapkido associates no traditional martial art weapons with its practice. It has, however, developed the use of the cane into a fine art form; making it not only a tool to aid in walking but a strategic defense weapon as well. It has elevated it from a simple piece of wood that can be swung randomly, to a conscious form of self defense.

The techniques of Hapkido make the cane one of the safest and most unimposing self-defense objects available. It only becomes dangerous when placed in the hands of a trained individual. Compared to other self-defense weapons, such as a gun or a knife, which are immediately considered deadly weapons by law enforcement, the cane, in terms of legality, does not possess that problem.

NOTE: The cane, or walking stick, is specifically for the purpose of fashion or assisting a person in walking. Its primary purpose is not as a bludgeon, and to carry a cane for this specific purpose may subject you to criminal penalties.

---

photographs by Joel Ciniero

The opponent launches a straight punch. It is blocked by the cane. The cane goes under the opponent's chin to throw him.

When one utilizes the cane as a weapon it not only increases one's striking distance and power (due to its reach and composition of wood or metal), but it can divert and trap on coming attacks as well. Imagine an adversary launches a punch; by performing an in-to-out block with the cane, it is easily deflected. The hooking handle of the cane can then easily lock around the opponent's neck as he is pulled down to be struck by your knee or simply thrown to the ground.

Modern Hapkido was developed by Choi Yong-shul in the early twentieth century. In 1910 he traveled to Japan and studied Daito-aikijujitsu. Many believe Hapkido to be a child of Aikido, but this is not the case. The late founder of Aikido, Morihei Uyeshiba, also studied at the Daito-aikijuitsu school. This is where the misunderstanding began.

Upon returning to Korea, Choi integrated the defensive mechanisms of the Japanese style with the strong kicking and punching techniques of the Korean martial art Tae Kyun. Hapkido, thus, incorporates the deflective moves commonly associated with Aikido and the forceful impact and counter strike potential of Tae Kyun into its cane techniques.

To better understand the self-defense potential of the

The techniques of Hapkido make the cane one of the safest and most effective self-defense objects around.

Hapkido cane, we need to view its various impact points and come to an understanding how this commonly seen object can be made into a self-defense instrument.

The cane has three main areas of offense and defense; they are: its length, (at its end), its handle, and its side. By isolating each area we may come to a deeper understanding of each of their potentials and proper usage.

The length of the cane (at its end) gives one the ability to strike an opponent at increased distances. It also allows one to keep an adversary held back, by maintaining the cane in a controlled outstretched fashion. This obviously is a great aid, in self defense and it could not be accomplished simply by the use of the hands or the feet.

This length gives one the time to educate one's opponents that they are not up against an average victim. It also allows one a moment of diversion to launch a further counterattack against an assailant.

The technique of striking with the end of the cane, when practiced, becomes quite focused; for example: the adversary is attempting a kick, the end of the cane strikes the leg, at the shin, ankle, or thigh region, thus holding back the attack. Then,

136

A punch is thrown by the opponent. It is blocked by the cane. A second punch is attempted by the opponent. The cane swings through and blocks it, as well. The opponent's neck is then locked by the cane's handle and he is thrown to the ground.

by continuing through, the opponent may be struck with the side of the cane.

The side of the cane can be swung baseball bat style, but it is far better to make the swinging impact more conscious so it cannot be easily deflected. If, however, the cane is unconsciously blocked by the opponent, the impact to the arm can have a equally debilitating effect. Any impacted strike with the cane does deliver an injury.

The side of the cane is first a striking device and secondly a trapping weapon; example: an oncoming punch is first blocked by the cane, then the side of the cane continues through wrapping around the arm of the opponent as he is pulled down to be kicked.

Though the handle of the cane can, of course, be used as an extension of the arm or as a striking device, its primary function is to be used in trapping. Once a block or a strike is performed, the hooking handle easily reaches around any bodily limb of the assailant to aid in the control of it. It is especially effective in grabbing at an opponent's neck.

It is elemental technique to Hapkido practitioners to use an adversary's own energy against him. This is accomplished by diverting any attack energy the opponent may launch and redirecting it to one's own advantage. The cane extends one's abilities in accomplishing this.

The idea is, of course, that instead of meeting an attack head on, it is far more effective to divert an opponent's attack rather than to simply attempt to block it directly. Thus, the opponent's expended energy can be used against himself and far less of a toll is taken upon the defender.

This is accomplished by using an opponent's own force and relative speed; thereby taking control of and unbalancing his actions or aggressions to the desired end result. This is achieved by having the ability to quickly change one's own positioning and while staying focused and grounded diverting the opponent's energies against himself.

The deflection of an opponent's energy is based in the common law of forward motion. A punch or a leg technique is launched; by deflecting its attack, while allowing its motion to

137

The opponent grabs from behind. He is struck in the solar plexus and pushed back. First, the cane's owner strikes the opponent, then pivoting through the cane is locked around the neck of the opponent and he is thrown to the ground.

continue through, the opponent inadvertently just continues to move through with the force of his own energy. The cane, thereby, aids in this end result of this energy manipulation. And, due to its make up, it keeps one from injuring oneself while deflecting the aggressive techniques.

Hapkido, infamous for its lock, traps, and throws, incorporates all of them into the usage of the cane. Due to its solid structure it gives one added control over an opponent as well as enhanced striking power. One does not need to be highly versed in the joint locking techniques of Hapkido to easily incorporate them into one's martial art abilities.

When an opponent grabs one's body, by first striking him with the cane and then locking the handle of the cane around one of his body parts, one's manipulation becomes easy. An example of this is when an adversary grabs one from behind: first strike him with the end of the cane; when he has been shoved back, pivot, locking the handle of the cane around his neck. They then may be quickly drawn down as you strike him in the face with your knee. Thus, the confrontation has immediately ended.

The pattern of self defense laid down for the use of the Hapkido cane is:

1) Hold the opponent a bay by a strike or a defensive shove.

2) If the attack continues, deflect it; either by blocking and diverting the energy of their aggressive motion or grab an

Hapkido is famous for its locks, traps and throws. All of these are incorporated into the cane techniques.

opponents limb; lock it, and force his release of your body.

3) Counter strike, for with out a final offensive move the assailant may continue his assault.

The third and final point is also a key element in Hapkido. Another factor which sets it apart from the basically defensive Aikido. After any defense has been completed and an opponent's attack or bodily grab has been disengaged, it is imperative that he be counter struck. Without that final blow, his assault on your person may continue.

To advance in the use of any weapon from simple random motions to properly executed techniques one must both physically and mentally engage in its practice. It is no different with the Hapkido cane. Of course, solo practice is useful; however, optimum knowledge will be gained when working with a partner and observing how the body reacts to the individual strikes, locks, and throws. While doing this one must keep in mind that every strike, with the cane, has the ability to injure even the friendliest opponent, and every lock and throw has the ability to break bones. It is advised to wear padding in strike zones and to gently practice the locks and throws until their motion is completely understood and perfected.

It is always best to have eye contact with an opponent while using the cane, thereby gaining the ability of witnessing oncoming attacks. This allows one to not have to guess at what may or may not be coming. It is for this reason that one always pivots to a frontal position to encounter the assailant, after any initial self-defense is rendered.

The Hapkido cane is a viable weapon for all assault situations and must be properly viewed as such. As many cultures view the carrying of a cane as a sign of stature, the martial artist may now too promote his stature while protecting his body.

ABOUT THE AUTHOR: Scott Shaw has contributed several articles to IK.

A front kick is attempted by the opponent. The kick is intercepted with the end of the cane, it is shoved back. The opponent is then struck in the head by the cane.

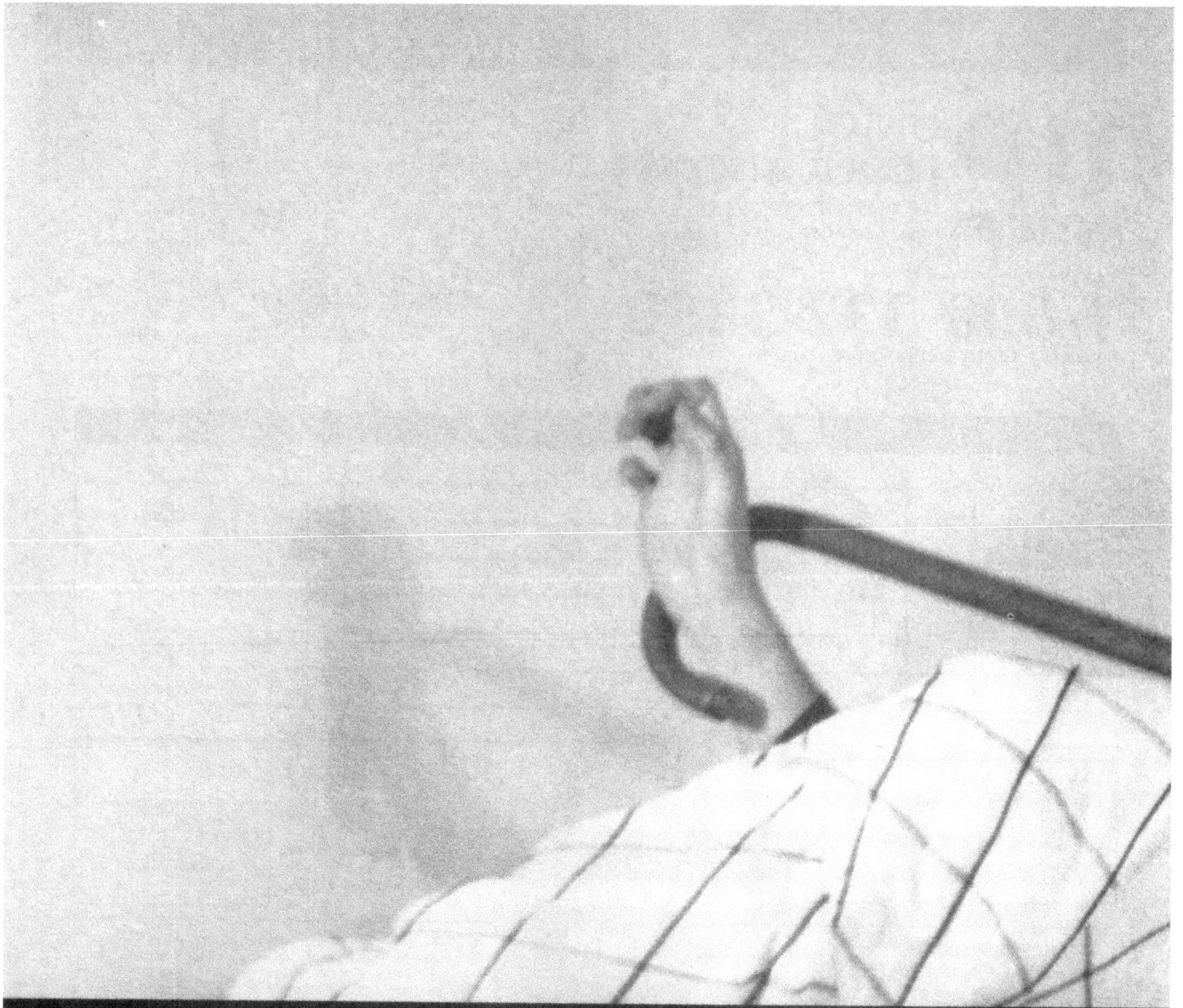

Body Locks And Throws

As time has progressed, the laws against martial art weaponry, even for personal safety, have virtually eliminated the use of all traditional weapons on the streets. There is one outstanding exception to those laws, however, the Hapkido cane. The common cane, found virtually everywhere, has been developed into a highly stylized and very useful self-defense weapon by the practitioners of the Korean martial art of Hapkido.

By Scott Shaw

Photos by Hae Won Shin

142

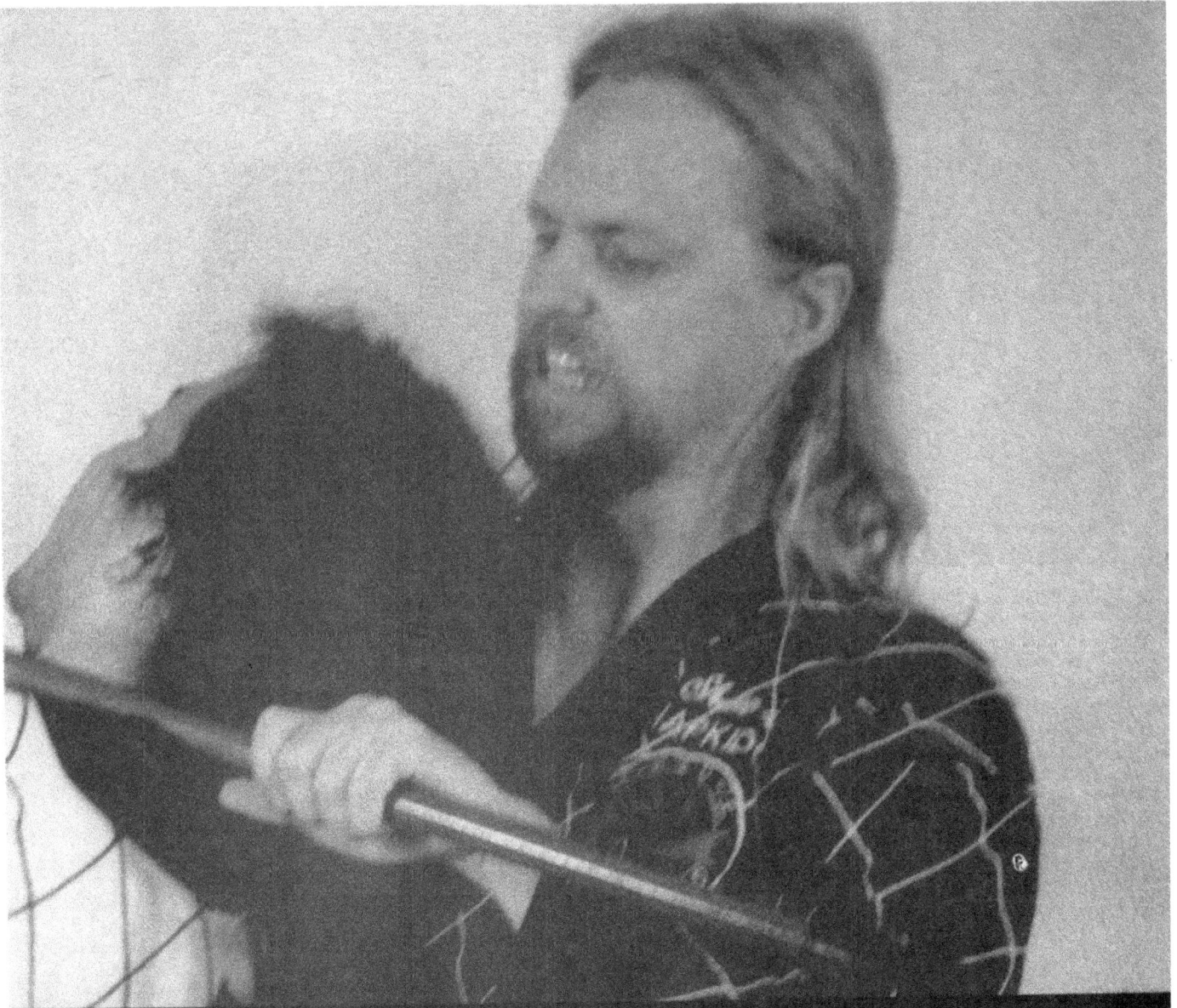

With The Hapkido Cane

Virtually anyone can randomly swing an object, such as the cane, and possibly strike an opponent. This type of random, haphazard, self-defense is never used in Hapkido, however. The reasoning behind this is because the results of that type of aimless self-defense are not calculable and to no one's advantage. Therefore, every movement which the practitioner of the Hapkido cane undertakes, is used in a fashion to give very specific and desired results; most prominently, suppression of your opponent's continuing attack on your body.

Hapkido practitioners, infamous for their joint-locking and throwing prowess, have taken their techniques a step further and incorporated these joint and body locks, which lead to throws with the use of the cane. To come to understand how one can success-fully lock an opponent into submission, we must first study the elemental rules of the Hapkido cane.

Joint-Locking Theory

First and foremost in joint-locking theory with the Hapkido cane is, you should never reach beyond a very short distance with the cane. This distance is approximately one half the overall length of the cane you are working with. By reaching beyond this distance, you can not maintain control over the cane. Thus, you give your opponent the ability to deflect the reaching cane and attack you further.

How, then, should you proceed to lock your opponent with the Hapkido cane? First of all, allow your opponent to travel within a

143

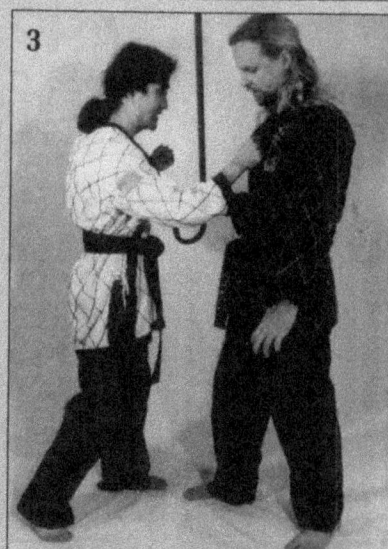

Your opponent grabs hold of you (1). You bring the Hapkido cane up and strike him in the groin (2). You then bring the cane over his exposed elbow and powerfully launch it into his elbow joint (3-4). His grasp is dislodged. Continuing through, you strike him in the head with the cane's handle and send him to the ground (5-6).

close proximity to your body — one to three feet. Thereby, he will have expended all of the energy in closing the distance between his body and yours.

Secondarily, once he has reached this close proximity to your body, allow him to make the initial attack. By allowing him to, once again, instigate the movements, you will witness what type of attack he is launching and thereby know what type of cane defense is best used to defend against it.

Also, by allowing your attacker to make the initial offensive movements, he is exposing the element of his body, which will be most easily controlled. For example, if he punches at you, his elbow is exposed. If he grabs hold of your clothing, his wrist, elbow, and neck are open and available to lock with the cane. By allowing him to make the first move, you will instantly know which body part you should direct your Hapkido cane body locks towards.

Prior to locking any element of your opponent's body, it is the Hapkido "rule-of-thumb" to strike your opponent with the cane, before you continue forward with any other defensive techniques. The focused hit with the cane will cause your opponent to be mo-

mentarily knocked off balance and his defenses will be opened up. This will allow you to more easily continue forward with effective body locking and throwing techniques.

As mentioned, the Hapkido cane is never swung randomly to battle your opponent. Therefore, once your opponent has instigated his attack, the cane's exacting movement can be sent to the appropriate location on your opponent's body to most effectively hinder his continued aggression. To achieve this, you will want to strike your opponent in the most debilitating location possible, at the instant you witness his oncoming attack.

Focused cane hits are accomplished by striking only to very specific locations on your opponent's body. For example, if your opponent is attacking you from the front, your ideal Hapkido cane strike points would be lifting the cane powerfully up into his groin, or striking him with the bottom end of the cane, forcefully, into his solar plexus or face. If he is attacking you from the rear, the bottom end of the cane can be powerfully driven into his solar plexus.

Once this initial cane strike is accomplished you can then effortlessly continue forward with additional defensive techniques.

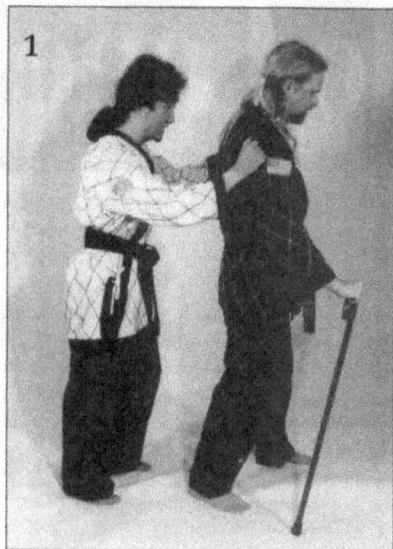

144

Continual Motion

Hapkido practices the theory of "Continual Motion" in all of its self-defense techniques. This is to say that you must continue forward, non-stop, from one technique immediately onto the next. This "Continual Motion" theory is practiced so that your opponent will not have the ability to successfully continue on with his own attack, if you successfully interrupt its progress. Thus, the initial strike, just discussed, gives you the ability to first stop his assault on you and then allow you the momentary time necessary, to continue on with your own defense.

In the case of your opponent attacking you from the front, once you have hit your opponent to one of these vital forward-strike locations, you must then immediately continue through locking his joints with the cane. The type of joint lock you will perform is governed by what type of forward attack he has launched at you. For example, if he has grabbed hold of your clothing, you can immediately rise the cane up and strike him in the groin.

Once this is accomplished, you will notice that the elbow of his grabbing arm is exposed. You can then, using both of your hands,

bring the length of the cane powerfully down across his elbow. This will not only disengage any hold he has on you, but you will have gained substantial control over his arm in the process. This will keep him from using that arm as a striking weapon.

Once his grip is free, you immediately continue the cane's movement by striking him in the head with the handle, as you continue forward with the power of the cane, sending him to the ground.

As we have seen, the Hapkido cane allows you to take advantage of exposed areas on your opponent's body and use them to your own advantage. This is the theory of all Hapkido joint-locking techniques.

You should never have to struggle to gain control over your opponent's joints. If you anticipate a muscle-to-muscle struggle, it is far better to use the cane against another area of your opponent's body which will be more easily controlled. For there is no advantage to adding to your confrontation by needlessly grappling.

Effective Joint-Locking

When using the Hapkido cane as a defensive weapon you do not have to rely on it solely for your self-defense. If your opponent

First and foremost in joint-locking theory with the Hapkido cane is, you should never reach beyond a very short distance with the cane. This distance is approximately one half the overall length of the cane you are working with. By reaching beyond this distance, you can not maintain control.

You are grabbed from behind (1). You strike your opponent to the solar plexus with the bottom end of the cane (2). Immediately, you pivot behind yourself and get him in a two-handed, cane choke hold (3-5).

145

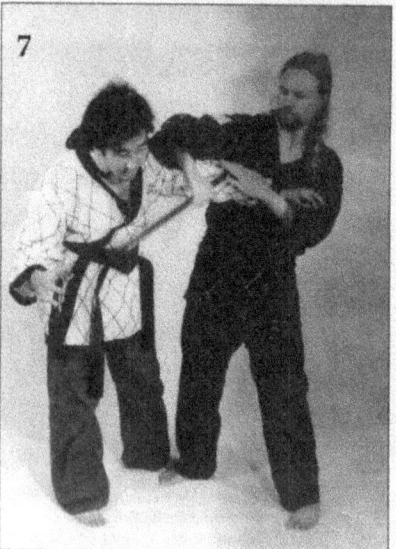

Your opponent punches at you (1). You block his advance with an out-to-in knife-hand block to his elbow region (2). Immediately, you strike him to his solar plexus with the cane (3). The cane's handle then comes down around his elbow (3-4). You spin the cane up and over your opponent's arm (5), as you step behind him (6). You lock the cane to your opponent's neck, as you send him back to the ground (7-8).

146

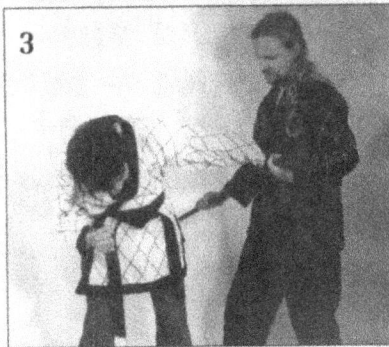

The opponent grabs your cane (1). You turn it over his arm, against his thumb (2-3). In the process, you lock the cane's handle around his wrist, as you send its length into his shoulder, body locking him (4).

Prior to locking any element of your opponent's body, it is the Hapkido "rule-of-thumb" to strike your opponent with the cane, before you continue forward with any other defensive techniques. The focused hit with the cane will cause your opponent to be momentarily knocked off balance and his defenses will be opened up.

comes forward at you with a straight punch, you can immediately block his attack with an out-to-in knife-hand block to his elbow region. Once you have achieved this initial halting of his attack, you can immediately strike your opponent to his solar plexus with the handle of your cane.

Now that his initial attack has been nullified and he is prone to effective joint-locking, due to the cane hit, you can then bring the handle of the cane down around his elbow. From this you will maintain virtual control over his arm. Now, by rapidly swinging the cane up and over his arm, you bring the cane across his throat. As you have simultaneously stepped behind his legs, you can now effortlessly throw him back and onto the ground.

If you are grabbed from behind, when you are in possession of a cane, you first counter defensive measure is always to strike your opponent, to not only loosen his hold on you but to hopefully injure him just enough that you can continue forward with effective defensive techniques.

As mentioned, if you are grabbed from behind, your ideal first-strike weapon, is to hit your opponent in his solar plexus with the bottom end of the cane. Once this initial strike is accomplished, you must rapidly move forward with additional defensive techniques so he will not have the ability to maintain his superior positioning behind you and launch a secondary attack.

Once you have hit your attacker with the cane in his solar plexus, his grasp will be loosened. By immediately pivoting, as you move the cane under and then over his grabbing arm, you will not only control his body to the point where it can not launch a successful secondary attack at you, but you will have opened him up for a powerful Hapkido cane body lock. This is accomplished by bringing the cane up to his neck level and holding him in a choke hold by grasping the cane at both ends, on either side of his head, until he surrenders.

Though the cane, when used properly, is a very effective street weapon, an adversary who is being defended against with it, may well attempt to take it away from you. Again, struggling muscle to muscle is never to your advantage. For this reason, if your opponent attempts to take control of your movements with the cane, you must immediately take it from his grasp.

Removing an opponent's grasp from the cane is quite easy. You must spin the cane circularly outward, thereby putting all of the cane's momentum driven power against the grasping thumb of your opponent.

Thumb as Weakest Point

One of the first lessons which is taught in Hapkido, is that the thumb is the weakest point of an opponent's grasp. It can not hold onto anything, when appropriate pressure is put against it. To this end, by spinning the cane outwards and placing its momentum on the thumb of your opponent, he will be instantly forced to let go of his grasp.

As you now understand, you should follow the "Continuous Motion" theory in all defensive undertakings. Therefore, once your opponent's grip has been dislodged from the cane, you must immediately follow through with additional defensive techniques to stop your opponent from assaulting you further.

It is always a good idea to follow one "Flow Path" from one technique onto the next. This is to say, your defenses with the Hapkido cane should go in a continuous pattern that allows you to easily move from one technique onto the next. They should not be haphazard, randomly alternating attempts at subduing your opponent. Therefore, as you are swinging the cane out and over your opponent's arm, dislodging his grasp, you should grab hold of the hand he grasps your cane with, while this grasp removal is in progress. By doing this, you then control the movement of that hand. Thus, not allowing it to pull free and possibly striking at you.

Once you have taken hold of his hand while the cane is in motion, you should twist his wrist, so the cane handle can easily joint lock it, once it has been freed from his grasp.

By continuing to swing the cane over his arm, you can then lock it in tight against his shoulder blade. As the cane's handle has now pivoted into the positioning of grasping his wrist, you now have him in an effective body lock.

As we have seen, the Hapkido cane is not simply a way of aiding someone who has trouble walking. It is, however, a very effective weapon in defending against an attacking opponent. ■

Scott Shaw of *Hermosa Beach, California is a black belt, an actor and a prolific writer.*

147

www.ingramcontent.com/pod-product-compliance
Lightning Source LLC
Chambersburg PA
CBHW080532090426

42733CB00015B/2558